EXPECT THE EXTRAORDINARY

EXPECT THE EXTRAORDINARY

Thinking in the Image of Christ

by
Jerry Savelle

Harrison House
Tulsa, Oklahoma

05 04 03 02 01   19 18 17 16 15 14 13 12 11 10 09 08 07 06 05 04 03 02

Expect the Extraordinary—
Thinking in the Image of Christ
ISBN 1-57794-305-8
Copyright © 2000 by Jerry Savelle
P.O. Box 748
Crowley, Texas 76036

Published by Harrison House, Inc.
P.O. Box 35035
Tulsa, Oklahoma 74153

CONTENTS

INTRODUCTION

Now is the time for you to expect the extraordinary in your life. In this book, I'm going to share a prophecy that was given to me in October 1998 that has revolutionized my life. I want you to take hold of it for your life as well as you read this book. Expect the extraordinary everywhere you are, everywhere you look and in everything you do. Realize that what once was rare is going to become the norm in your life.

This prophecy is to be taken seriously. It is your responsibility to receive the prophecy and to act upon it. This book will teach you how to do just that. If you accept this challenge, your life will never be the same. Your existence will no longer be ordinary, and you will begin to live an extraordinary life. People will be drawn to you as you experience miracles performed in extraordinary ways, and you will be able to witness to them about the special blessings of God. The manifestations of the extraordinary in your life will establish the supremacy of God in their hearts.

This book is written to challenge you to take the limits off God. Learn to stand in faith. Forget the past, because "usual" is no longer the norm.

We are the result of what we believe. What do *you* believe? Do you realize that you are God's special treasure? It's time to get a revelation of who you are in

Christ. You are approved of God. You are one of God's greatest creations.

Some of the questions that will be addressed in this book are:

- How do I get in position to receive what God can do in my life?

- Am I willing to do what it takes to achieve the extraordinary?

- Am I willing to have a listening ear to hear God's instructions to me?

- How is God going to repay Satan for all the things he's robbed me of?

I encourage you to read *Expect the Extraordinary* with an open heart and with a willingness to follow the principles set forth in the following pages. As you do this, you will position yourself to receive the extraordinary in every area of your life. So get ready for one of the greatest adventures you have ever embarked on in your walk with the Lord!

BIBLICAL PRINCIPLES OF PROPHECY

Before I share with you the prophecy that was given to me in October 1998 and its significance to the body of Christ, I want to define what prophecy is.

According to *Vine's Expository Dictionary of Biblical Words,* the word *prophecy* is defined as "the speaking forth of the mind and counsel of God."[1]

Prophecy is not meant to be used as "fortune telling." Prophecy is not meant to be used by the false prophet to manipulate people into doing the will of another human being.

True prophecy is when a messenger or representative of God proclaims the will of God which cannot be known by or through natural means. The prophecy can have reference to the past, the present or the future.[2]

The purpose of prophecy is to encourage, to edify and to comfort believers. Prophecy may be given to an individual and may address a specific situation that pertains to that one person. Many times this kind of prophecy is given in private and is meant for the ears of the recipient only. Other times, it is meant to publicly encourage the believer. This happens frequently in prayer lines, or even while the messenger is delivering a sermon.

Sometimes a prophecy is given to an unbeliever, and through that prophecy, the person is directed to God and brought to a saving knowledge of Jesus Christ.

Prophecy may also be given to the body of Christ in general. These prophecies may be given publicly to a large audience, or they may be given to an individual who then passes that word on to others. Again, whether given to an individual or to a greater number of people, the prophecy is to encourage, to edify and to comfort.

Prophecy is to be taken very seriously and reverently as it is a Word given under the unction of the Holy Spirit.

Chapter 1

Taking Prophecy Seriously

In his first letter to Timothy, the apostle Paul writes:

> This charge I commit unto thee, son Timothy, according to the prophecies which went before on thee, that thou by them mightest war a good warfare; holding faith, and a good conscience; which some having put away concerning faith have made shipwreck.
>
> 1 Timothy 1:18,19

In verse 18, Paul is admonishing and charging his son in the Lord, Timothy, to take heed to the prophecies that have been prophesied over him and by them war a good warfare. *The Amplified Bible* says, **inspired and aided by them you may wage the good warfare.**

In other words, we are not to take prophecy lightly.

Question the Vessel

Unfortunately—particularly in our day—people get up in a church service, point their fingers in the air, shout in tongues and say, "Thus saith the Lord!" But sometimes we wonder whether this "prophecy" is really from God. Sometimes we question the vessel that it's coming through.

I remember years ago when Brother Kenneth Copeland and I were in El Paso, Texas, in a Full Gospel Businessmen's Convention. Of course, I was young in the Lord then, and I was still learning.

The congregation would pause between the song service and the sermon and wait a long time, hoping there might be a word from God. And if nobody gave one, then someone would come up with one!

That used to bother me. I'd think, *If God wanted to say something, He could have thought of it by now*. But they just kept pausing for longer and longer periods of time. Finally somebody felt compelled to give a word—and usually it would be off the wall.

That's what happened in this meeting in El Paso. There was a long pause, and finally a lady stood up and said, "Thus saith the Lord: Having a wonderful time. Wish you were here."

Well, I had a hard time believing that came from God. I think that just came out of her head and was not necessarily inspired by the Holy Spirit!

I remember another time when a prophecy was given. A woman stood up and said, "Thus saith the Lord: Was I not with Joshua when I split the Red Sea? Was I not with Joshua when I led the people out of Egypt? Was I not with Joshua when I got water out of a rock? Was I not with Joshua when...." Suddenly she stopped and then said, "The Lord hath made a mistake. It wasn't Joshua; it was Moses." Well, when you hear things like that, you begin to question whether some of these prophecies are really from God!

Another time, I heard a woman prophesy over a church that she thought was out of order. And she said, "Thus saith the Lord: God shall write *Michelob* on thy walls." Of course, she meant *Ichabod,* but she said *Michelob.* Well, when you hear off-the-wall, goofy things like that, you can be sure they're not from God!

Keep the Antenna Up

The danger of this sort of thing is that if we're not careful, then we'll take lightly or ignore it when God actually does say something prophetic to us.

For example, when someone like Kenneth Hagin says, "Thus saith the Lord," my spiritual antenna goes up. I believe Brother Hagin to be accurate in the Holy Ghost. I believe him to be a prophet of God. Therefore, when he declares something by the Spirit of God, then he's got my attention.

But I've been in meetings in years past in which Brother Hagin was prophesying and people were doing all kinds of things—unwrapping gum, flipping through the Bible, talking to one another or even getting up and walking around. Yet God was speaking!

Perhaps that's the reason why some people say about their personal prayer lives, "God doesn't talk to me very much." Could it be that God doesn't talk to you because you don't listen very well? Could it be that we're not listening very well as a church?

Prophecy from God is not to be taken lightly. The apostle Paul tells Timothy that prophecies which have been spoken over you are to be used to wage a good spiritual warfare. And as *The Amplified Bible* says, those prophecies are to inspire and aid you.

Doing Our Part

Now, a lot of people have the idea that if God prophesies something, it will just come to pass automatically, without our having to do anything about it. But if that were true, why would Paul tell Timothy to use prophecy to **war the good warfare?**

Kenneth Hagin has laid hands on my wife, Carolyn, and me and prophesied over us and our ministry. Oral Roberts has done this a number of times. So has Kenneth Copeland. These are all great men of God, and I have complete confidence in their ability to hear God. They have prophesied over me—not once, but many times.

If it's been in a setting where the prophecy has been recorded, I immediately get the tape and have it transcribed. Then I carry that word around with me everywhere I go. It stays in my notebook. And every time I think about it, I pull it out and read it and remind the devil of it. If I'm facing circumstances that look contrary to what's been prophesied over me, I pull it out, and I declare, "It is written." To me, that prophecy is Holy Writ. It was inspired by God.

My Responsibility

Back in 1969 when I first came to the Lord, Brother Kenneth Copeland was preaching in the church where my wife, Carolyn, grew up. I was sitting there listening to him when all of a sudden, right in the middle of his sermon, he just stopped and said, "Jerry, stand up."

Well, it really surprised me that he even remembered my name. I'd only met him a few months before.

He said, "Jerry, stand up."

I stood up, and he said, "God just showed me that you and I will become a team, and we will preach the Gospel together around the world for the rest of our lives. And it will be your responsibility to believe God for the perfect timing."

Then he told me to be seated, and he took up where he left off and kept preaching.

Now, I've been associated with Kenneth Copeland for over thirty years and I can remember just about every sermon he's ever preached in my presence—except that one! I don't remember another word he said after that because all I could think about was, *We're going to become a team? We're going to preach the Word together around the world for the rest of our lives?*

That's the last thing I heard in that service. And I carried that word around with me everywhere I went. I wrote it down in my notebook. I wrote it down in my Bible, dated it and expected it to come to pass.

However, I had sense enough to realize that when he said, "It will be your responsibility to believe God for the perfect timing," this wasn't going to just come to pass automatically unless I did my part.

Remember, Paul says that when a prophecy is spoken over you, you are to take that prophecy and war a good warfare with it. It was spoken to inspire you and to be an aid to you.

I've carried around prophecies that Brother Copeland has spoken over me through the years and watched them come to pass as a result of Carolyn's and my standing in faith for them. The primary reason I'm saying this is that I want to build a foundation to lead into a prophecy we're going to be talking about in the rest of this book.

A Prophecy for the Days Ahead

In October 1998, I heard the Spirit of God say this: *Beginning in 1999, I will do for you what you've tried to do yourself but could not do. I will cause to come to pass those things which you've strived for and tried to accomplish in your own strength and in your own might but just could not make them happen. I will bring them to pass for you. Extraordinary things will become the norm in your life. Things that never happened to most people in a lifetime will happen to you in one year's time. It's time to expect the extraordinary.*

I believe that this is a word from God for all of us. God is saying that we need to begin to look for the extraordinary.

The Meaning of Extraordinary

Since God said that extraordinary things would become the norm, I decided that I'd look up the word *extraordinary* in my dictionary. And here's what I discovered about this word. It means "beyond the common order, beyond the common method and beyond the common course of things."[1] The second definition that I discovered was "remarkable, uncommon and rare."[2] To me that meant that God was saying, *What once was rare is going to become the norm.*

God was telling me that breakthroughs in prayer, in finances, in healing and in the restoration of relationships that once were rare, were going to become common— not only in my life, but in the lives of the entire body of Christ who would dare believe for them.

I began preaching this everywhere I went, and often people would say, "I just can't imagine that." God knows that some people will have a hard time believing that extraordinary things can happen to them. In fact, He mentions this in the Bible.

A Work You Wouldn't Believe

For example, speaking through the mouth of the prophet Habakkuk, God says,

> **Behold ye among the heathen, and regard, and wonder marvellously: for I will work a work in your days, which ye will not believe, though it be told you.**
>
> **Habakkuk 1:5**

God said that in Habakkuk's day He was going to work a work that would be so marvelous, so wonderful, so extraordinary that some people would not be able to believe it. He repeats this statement in the apostle Paul's day.

> **Behold, ye despisers, and wonder, and perish: for I work a work in your days, a work which ye shall in no wise believe, though a man declare it unto you.**
>
> **Acts 13:41**

The Amplified Bible says in the latter part of that verse, **even if someone clearly describing it in detail**

declares it to you. The fact that God said this both in Habakkuk's day and in Paul's day leads me to believe that God is saying this to every generation.

God is saying, *I am going to work a work in your day that will be so marvelous, so wonderful, so extraordinary that some will not be able to believe it, even if it is clearly described to them in detail.*

When God makes statements like this, we need to realize that it's time for us to stretch our faith, stretch our imaginations and think bigger than we've ever thought before. In the rest of this book, I'm going to show you how the extraordinary can become the norm in your life.

Chapter 2

A New Thing

I said in the last chapter that God told me that beginning in 1999, extraordinary things would become the norm. Once again, the word *extraordinary* means "beyond the common order, beyond the common method and beyond the common course of things." It also means "remarkable, uncommon and rare."

The Usual Method

If you are employed, then the usual method of having your life sustained and your needs met on a daily basis is through your paycheck. You work a certain number of hours each week or month, and then you are given a paycheck. And with that paycheck you pay your mortgage. You pay your car payment. You buy groceries. You keep your children clothed. You put food on your table.

So the common method for having your life sustained is by your getting up every morning, going to work, doing what you're supposed to do and then receiving a check for your work at the end of a certain period of time. But when God says, *I'm going to do the extraordinary,* He's saying, *Don't limit Me to your paycheck!*

You see, I believe there are people reading this book who are going to learn about some inheritances they didn't know they had coming. Why not? You might have a distant relative you haven't seen in years who will leave you an inheritance.

This has happened in our ministry. Occasionally, we find out that people have put our ministry in their wills. Every once in a while, we'll get a notification from an attorney stating that someone passed away, and they had designated a certain amount of their estate to go into our ministry. And we didn't even know it. We had no idea that they had included us.

Why couldn't that happen to you? "Well, Brother Jerry," you say, "I just don't know anybody in our family who might leave me some money. So that's highly improbable."

How about bonuses you didn't expect? How about raises you didn't know you had coming? How about promotions that you thought you wouldn't get because you thought you didn't have enough seniority? You may wonder why you got that position instead of the person who seemed to be in line for it. Maybe it's because that person doesn't know God and you do.

High Expectations

What I'm saying is that God wants us to get our expectations as high as we possibly can. God wants to do things that are so extraordinary that some people are not going to be able to believe it. But if you'll stand in faith for it and take His prophecies seriously, expecting them to come to pass, then the extraordinary will become the norm in your life.

Supernatural Increase

Why couldn't God do this for *you?* What do you have to lose by expecting God's prophecies to come true? Let me give you another example.

In November 1992, the Lord told me that He was going to teach me the keys to supernatural increase and restoration, and that I was to preach it everywhere I went. In February 1993, I preached for three nights in a friend's church on this subject. On the last night, I laid hands on everyone in the building and commanded supernatural increase and restoration into their lives.

Three days later, after the meeting was over, I received a call from my friend.

He said, "Jerry, our ministry is celebrating our first ten years, and we have just had the greatest financial miracle that we've ever had! One of the men you laid hands on called me this morning and wanted to know if he could bring me the tithe from his supernatural increase. I met him at my office, and when he walked in the door, he held out a check for $1.2 million. He told me that this was his tithe from his supernatural increase—which means that this man had just received $12 million!"

I said, "Do me a favor. I have never seen a check for a $1.2 million tithe. I know you're telling the truth and you wouldn't exaggerate, but would you mind making a copy of that check? When I come back I'd like to see it."

He said, "Of course."

So later in the year, I went back to his church, and not only did he show me the copy of the check for the $1.2 million tithe, but he had the man who gave it come into his office before the service. The man gave me the testimony of how his supernatural increase came about.

When I saw that $1.2 million check, the Spirit of God said, *What is rare now will become the norm before the appearing of Jesus.*

Forget the Past

So God wants us to begin to expect the extraordinary. Forget about the past, and don't limit God by saying, "I've never heard anything like this before in my life." Don't say that. That doesn't have anything to do with what God's going to do in the future. You haven't seen everything God can do, but if you'll dare to believe, then you will!

In fact, His Word says:

> **Do not [earnestly] remember the former things; neither consider the things of old. Behold I am doing a new thing.**
>
> **Isaiah 43:18,19** AMP

God is doing a new thing. And if God wants to do a new thing, then let Him do it! He says in Isaiah 43:13 AMP, **I will work, and who can hinder or reverse it?** God is saying, "I'm going to do this. Satan's not going to be able to stop it. Governments are not going to be able to stop it. Politicians won't be able to stop it. The economy won't be able to stop it." God is actually saying that it's going to happen and you can either expect it to come to pass in your life or just hear about it happening to others. It's coming anyway.

It's a new thing. Satan is not going to be able to stop it. This is the beginning of the extraordinary, the remarkable, the rare.

I began to tell congregations everywhere to look on each new day as another day for the extraordinary to happen in their lives. What you couldn't do yourself before, expect God to do each day. Expect what everyone else says is rare to happen to you all the time. I told them to say, "I'm not normal. I'm living in the realm of the extraordinary."

Extraordinary Miracles

And God wrought special miracles by the hands of Paul: so that from his body were

**brought unto the sick handkerchiefs or aprons,
and the diseases departed from them, and the
evil spirits went out of them.**

Acts 19:11,12

The Amplified Bible translates the phrase *special miracles* as **unusual and extraordinary miracles.** In other words, this was not the norm. Something began to happen in Paul's life that was not the norm. Clothing that touched his body was put on other people who were sick or demon possessed. And whenever those pieces of cloth were placed upon people, those people were made whole and delivered. This was extraordinary. It was not the norm.

Paul always experienced miracles in his ministry. But then he entered into a new thing that had not been happening to him before.

I've had miracles in my life and ministry. But what I hear God saying is, *I'm going to do miracles in the days ahead which you've never seen done quite this way before.*

Of course, every miracle is extraordinary. How could you say anything else about a miracle? But God is saying, *The way I performed the miracles you've seen in the past*

*is not the only way I can perform them. I'm going to show
you new ways in the days ahead.*

Coming Back Big Time

Brother Oral Roberts sat in my home one night and
said that God had visited him and told him that healing
and miracles are coming back to the body of Christ *big
time.* He said that he'd experienced many miracles in his
ministry—back when he was conducting tent crusades
across America—but God was about to do some things
that would be greater than anything he'd seen in the past.

Then he described what happened in a service under
the big tent in which the anointing of God suddenly
swept through the place. Every sick person and every
demon-possessed person was healed instantly without
his laying hands on anyone. The *shekinah* glory of God
filled that tent. Everybody fell on the floor. And when
they got up, they were all healed and delivered!

Brother Roberts said that God had been telling him
that these kinds of extraordinary occurrences were
coming back *big time.* It won't be uncommon. It's going

to start happening more and more frequently. What once was rare is going to become the norm.

Who Will Get It?

Before we go on, let me say that it is God's will that every member of His family experience these extraordinary miracles. It is the will of God that every member of the body of Christ experience these things. However, not every member will.

You may say, "If it's the will of God, then it will just happen."

Oh, is that right? Well, it's the will of God that all men be saved and come into the knowledge of the truth. Yet there are many people going to hell. So if it's just automatic, then why are there some who will go to hell?

Unfortunately, hell is not an empty place. Why? Because some people will not appropriate God's will in their lives.

Why It Won't Happen to Everyone

Now you might be asking, "Is God going to do extraordinary things for everybody in the body of Christ?"

The answer is no. This is not going to happen to everybody in the body of Christ. Why not? And who *will* it happen to? Who will experience these extraordinary things in their lives in the years ahead? We can find part of the answer in what Jesus said to some blind men who asked Him to heal them.

The gospel of Matthew tells us why the extraordinary will not happen to everyone.

> **And when Jesus departed thence, two blind men followed him, crying, and saying, Thou Son of David, have mercy on us. And when he was come into the house, the blind men came to him: and Jesus saith unto them, Believe ye that I am able to do this? They said unto him, Yea, Lord.**
>
> **Matthew 9:27,28**

So here's the question: Do you believe He is able to do this? Do you believe He is able to bring the extraordinary to pass in your life?

Let me ask you another question. Was it God's will to heal these blind men who came to Jesus? Of course it was His will to heal them.

But notice that Jesus turned the responsibility to receive over to them. It was the will of God for them to be healed—Jesus proved that everywhere He went in his earthly ministry. Everywhere He went, He healed and delivered people.

So there's no doubt as to whether it was the will of God for these men to be healed. But notice that they were not healed automatically just because it was the will of God. If they were going to experience this miracle in their lives, they had to take responsibility. Jesus put the responsibility for the manifestation of the miracle back on them.

He's doing the same thing with you and me. If we are going to see the extraordinary become the norm, then we must take the responsibility for expecting God's prophetic word to come to pass.

According to Their Faith

When the blind men asked Jesus to restore their sight, He asked them if they believed He could perform the miracle that they had asked for. And they said **Yea, Lord** (Matt. 9:28).

Then touched he their eyes, saying, According to your faith be it unto you. And their eyes were opened.

Matthew 9:29,30

Those who believe He is able to do it will receive miracles. I love the way *The Message* translation reads in these verses: **Jesus said to them, "Do you really believe I can do this?" They said, "Why, yes, Master!" He touched their eyes and said, "Become what you believe."**

Become What You Believe

My friends, I am today what I believed about myself yesterday. And I'm going to be tomorrow what I believe about myself today. Everything I'm doing right now, everything Carolyn and I possess, everything this ministry is about and everything this ministry is doing is a result of what we believed.

This is not a coincidence with us. It's not because we were born under some lucky star. No, we believed God, and everything we're doing right now is the result of how we have believed.

If I had listened to the "religious" people thirty years ago—if I had believed what they thought about me—I would have never gotten my ministry off the ground. But I chose not to believe what they thought. I chose to believe what I was hearing God say. I chose to believe what I saw in the Word. And as a result of it, I am today what I believed yesterday. I will be tomorrow what I am believing today. I am what I believe!

And so are you. If you don't like the way your life has turned out, then change what you believe about yourself and your life!

God's Purpose for Doing the Extraordinary

Before we go too much further on getting in position to experience the extraordinary, I want us to determine first of all why God would want to do this. Why does God want us to experience extraordinary things in our lives? Why does He want the rare to become the norm? Is it just so you and I can have our needs met? Is it just so we can live a comfortable Christian lifestyle?

No, I think God's purpose runs deeper than that. Anytime God does something special for you, it's because

He's got something additional on His mind. So let's find out *why* God wants you to experience what once was uncommon and rare to become the norm in your life.

The answer is found in the book of Acts.

Now Peter and John went up together into the temple at the hour of prayer, being the ninth hour.

And a certain man lame from his mother's womb was carried, whom they laid daily at the gate of the temple which is called Beautiful, to ask alms of them that entered into the temple; who seeing Peter and John about to go into the temple asked an alms. And Peter, fastening his eyes upon him with John, said, Look on us.

And he gave heed unto them, expecting to receive something of them.

Then Peter said, Silver and gold have I none; but such as I have give I thee: in the name of Jesus Christ of Nazareth, rise up and walk. And he took him by the right hand, and lifted him up: and immediately his feet and ankle bones received strength. And he leaping up stood, and walked, and entered with them into the temple, walking, and leaping, and praising God.

And all the people saw him walking and praising God: and they knew that it was he which sat for alms at the Beautiful gate of the temple: and they were filled with wonder and amazement at that which had happened unto him.

Acts 3:1-10

Now, it is obvious that the people who saw this man walking and leaping realized something uncommon and rare had happened. This man had been carried to that gate every day, all of his life. He was a beggar. In those days, beggars wore particular apparel that identified them as beggars. They wore beggars' robes.

This man's normal begging place was at the gate called Beautiful. There were people going in and out of that gate all day long. They had watched this man sit there for years. His presence there was, as we say, "old hat." Nobody who went in and out of that gate was surprised when they saw him there.

A Customary Sight

This story in the Bible reminds me of a man in a little community near where I grew up. This man was mentally handicapped. He had the mentality of a child, and he would dress up in a cowboy costume with toy guns and stand out in the street, pretending to direct traffic. Since he did this every day for years, no one in town was surprised by it. We just got accustomed to him. People who knew him by name would call to him and wave at him as they drove by. They were so used to seeing him there that they no longer thought that there was anything strange or unusual about it.

Well, I believe this man at the gate called Beautiful was in the same situation. He was there every day. When people walked by, they saw him. When they walked by, he had his hands up and was asking for alms. So there was nothing uncommon about this particular day. Same routine, same story—it was nothing uncommon.

And you may not have thought about this, but it is probable that this man sat at that gate every day during Jesus' ministry. Jesus went through that gate a few times. Why didn't the man get healed then? We know that it is the will of God to heal.

The Healer himself walked by that man, but the Bible never mentions that Jesus ministered to him or even spoke to him. He may have, but the Bible doesn't mention it.

But here in Acts—on one of those normal days—this same man, at the same gate, with the same people walking through that gate, experienced something extraordinary. What happened? Peter and John came through the gate, and the man began begging alms as usual. And they looked at him and commanded him, "Look on us." And he did. Then Peter said, **Silver and gold have I none; but such as I have, give I thee.** Something happened when the man heard that. The disciples didn't have what he asked for, but something happened on the inside of him.

An Expectancy of Something

What happened? Suddenly the man had an expectancy of something. He didn't know what it was, but he knew he was going to get something. When Peter said, "We don't have what you think you want, but what we do have we're going to give you," the beggar had no idea that it was going to be the name of Jesus. But he knew it was *something*—and when a beggar knows he's going to get something, he reaches his hand out even farther.

If you have ever been to a third-world country where begging is common, then you know what I'm talking about. So he was reaching out, expecting something. And Peter said, **In the name of Jesus Christ of Nazareth, rise up and walk.**

At that moment, something extraordinary happened in this man's life. He was completely healed and miraculously restored to health, and he jumped up and began to leap and praise God.

Well now, when these people are walking by, seeing a man leaping and praising God, they know something extraordinary has happened. But let me ask you this question: Did this extraordinary thing that happened to this man end with him? No, it did not. God had something on His mind that was going to affect other people as well.

In the next chapter, the Bible says, **Howbeit many of them which heard the word believed** (Acts 4:4).

Now, remember, the religious people called Peter and John "on the carpet" for this. They told them to stop preaching in the name of Jesus. But they went on preaching anyway. Peter said, "We're going to obey God and not men."

And the Bible says five thousand men believed the Word.

What happened? An extraordinary thing happening in the life of one person affected five thousand people. You see, the reason God wants you and me to experience the extraordinary is because He wants to use that experience to get the attention of others.

God has a purpose much deeper, much broader, than just making your life nice and comfortable.

The Effect on Others

Now don't get me wrong, God *is* interested in making your life better. In fact, He wants you to live an abundant life. But His ultimate purpose is deeper than that. He wants what's happening to you to affect multitudes of other people.

Folks, we are rapidly approaching the appearing of Jesus. We're not talking about a hundred years from now. He's coming. It's possible that it will happen in our generation. We're the generation that could witness this great event. The stage is being set right now.

And that's why the miraculous, the extraordinary, the unusual and the special are going to intensify from here on out: it will be used as a tool for evangelism. That's what the extraordinary is all about.

Chapter 3

The Next Level

So far, we have been defining the *extraordinary* as "beyond the common order, beyond the common method and beyond the common course of things." However, as I studied and prayed about what God had said to me, I discovered some additional meanings which I think will help take your faith for the extraordinary to a higher level.

An additional meaning of *extraordinary* is "a work wrought by a divine power for a divine purpose by means beyond the reach of common man."[1] In other words, man can't do it. It's beyond his reach. It takes a supreme being to do what we're talking about here.

Second, the extraordinary is "an event or effect in the physical world deviating from the known laws of nature."[2]

Third, it means "an abnormal event brought about by supreme means."[3]

Fourth, the extraordinary is "a work out of the usual sequence of causes and effects which cannot be accounted for by the ordinary operation of those causes."[4]

There is a law of cause and effect. That means that if you do something the same way every time, you're going to get the same results. But when extraordinary things happen, then it becomes a work out of the usual sequence of cause and effect which cannot be accounted for other than by God.

The extraordinary can also be defined as something "transcending the ordinary."[5]

And finally, it is "the reversal of natural laws or the reversal of the natural course of things."[6] If God wants to do the extraordinary, He is willing to reverse natural laws to do it if that's what it takes.

The Power of Control

Now before you say, "Come on, Brother Jerry! God can't change the laws of nature," pay close attention to this statement: *Since God is the maker of natural laws, He has the power to control, change, suspend or redirect them as He deems necessary.* God made natural laws, and He can change them at His will. He can control them or redirect them at His will.

Manifestations of the extraordinary establish the supremacy of God. That's why He wants to do the extraordinary—because no one else can! Colossians 1:16 says,

For by him were all things created, that are in heaven, and that are in earth, visible and invisible, whether they be thrones, or dominions, or principalities, or powers: all things were created by him, and for him.

So that means everything is under His control. He can change natural laws if He deems it necessary. If He wants to change a natural law, override a natural law or redirect a natural law—if that's what it takes to meet your need and prove to you that He is supreme—then He can do it as He deems necessary.

Let's look at what Psalm 102:25-27 says about this:

Of old hast thou laid the foundation of the earth: and the heavens are the work of thy hands.

They shall perish, but thou shalt endure: yea, all of them shall wax old like a garment; as a vesture shalt thou change them, and they shall be changed:

But thou art the same, and thy years shall have no end.

What is the psalmist saying? He is telling us that God created everything, and even though heaven and earth may perish, He shall endure forever. In other words, creation will never become greater than the Creator. So that means if it is necessary to change, redirect, control or override something in the natural course of things in order to meet your need, then He reserves the right to do so.

And it sounds to me like God is saying, *If you'll raise your expectations and if you'll dare believe that I can do this, then I'm going to show you, from here until the appearing of Jesus, unusual, extraordinary demonstrations of My ability like you've never seen before.*

His One Command

By performing extraordinary miracles in our lives, God shows Himself alive. He shows Himself in control of anything that would attempt to prevent us from enjoying everything that He has promised we can have. When the extraordinary happens in your life, it becomes infallible proof that He is alive.

Now read this carefully. God's command to us, no matter what our circumstances may be, is simply this: **Only believe.**

Isn't that what Jesus told Jairus?

> **And when Jesus was passed over again by ship unto the other side, much people gathered unto him: and he was nigh unto the sea.**
>
> **And, behold, there cometh one of the rulers of the synagogue, Jairus by name; and when he saw him, he fell at his feet, and besought him greatly, saying, My little daughter lieth at the point of death: I pray thee, come and lay thy hands on her, that she may be healed; and she shall live.**
>
> **And Jesus went with him; and much people followed him, and thronged him.**

And a certain woman, which had an issue of blood twelve years, and had suffered many things of many physicians, and had spent all that she had, and was nothing bettered, but rather grew worse, when she had heard of Jesus, came in the press behind, and touched his garment. For she said, If I may touch but his clothes, I shall be whole.

And straightway the fountain of her blood was dried up; and she felt in her body that she was healed of that plague.

And Jesus, immediately knowing in himself that virtue had gone out of him, turned him about in the press, and said, Who touched my clothes?

And his disciples said unto him, Thou seest the multitude thronging thee, and sayest thou, Who touched me?

And he looked round about to see her that had done this thing. But the woman fearing and trembling, knowing what was done in her, came and fell down before him, and told him all the truth.

And he said unto her, Daughter, thy faith hath made thee whole; go in peace, and be whole of thy plague.

While he yet spake, there came from the ruler of the synagogue's house certain which

**said, Thy daughter is dead: why troublest thou
the Master any further?**

**As soon as Jesus heard the word that was
spoken, he saith unto the ruler of the synagogue,
Be not afraid, only believe.**

Mark 5:21-36

Jairus's daughter was dying. In fact, before Jesus got
to the man's house, she did die.

But did you notice that Jesus didn't turn to him and
say, "Well, if I hadn't been held up by this woman with the
issue of blood, we'd have gotten there on time. I'm sorry. I
wish there had been something we could have done."
But He didn't. He turned immediately and said, "Don't be
afraid. Only believe."

Jesus heard the report that in the natural course of
things, the girl had already died. But it didn't shake Jesus
at all. Why? He's in control. He can change the natural
course of things.

The Wrong Question

All God is commanding us to do is simply to believe.
The same command Jesus gave Jairus becomes our
command today: **Only believe.**

What was the question God asked Sarah, knowing it was impossible for her to conceive and to give birth? He asked, **Is any thing too hard for the Lord?** (Gen. 18:14).

Our question should never be, "*Can* God?" Our question should be, "How do I get in position to receive what God can do?" It's not a question of God's ability. My question to God is never, "Can You?" My question is not even, "Will You?" Because I know that since He can, He will. It's not a question of if God can or will—He can and will!

The question is this: How do I get in position to receive? How do I get in position to receive the extraordinary?

The Basic Law of the Planet

To answer this question, we need to know the primary law by which this planet and our lives operate. We find this law at the very beginning of the story of creation.

> **And God said, Behold, I have given you**
> **every herb bearing seed, which is upon the face**
> **of all the earth, and every tree, in the which is**
> **the fruit of a tree yielding seed; to you it shall**
> **be for meat.**
>
> **Genesis 1:29**

Every seed produces after its own kind. In other words, to get apples, you have to plant apple seeds. To get oranges, you have to plant orange seeds. If you want tomatoes, you have to plant tomato seeds. *And if you want the extraordinary, you have to be willing to plant an extraordinary seed. You have to be willing to do something that is above and beyond the norm of your life.*

Are We Willing?

You see, we all want the extraordinary, but are we willing to do what it takes to achieve it?

Let me give you an example. We are never going to experience a greater level of the glory of God coming into a service, filling the room like a cloud, if all we ever do is what we're doing right now in our praise and worship. If all we do is sing three songs, say "hallelujah" three times and "glory" once, then we won't experience it! We have to be willing to go to the next plateau in our praise and worship.

This is not true only in a church setting, but in our own individual lives as well. If you want the glory of God to come down in your prayer room, you're going to have to do something this year that you didn't do last year. Every seed produces after its own kind.

If you want the extraordinary, then you're going to have to get out of the norm. You may be further along this year than you were last year. But even if you are, there's another plateau. It doesn't end where you are now!

Extraordinary Giving

Do you want the extraordinary in your finances? Well then, are you willing to do something extraordinary where your finances are concerned? You cannot keep giving the same amount to God this year that you did last year and expect the extraordinary in your finances in the years ahead.

How do I get in position to receive the extraordinary? I must be willing to do something extraordinary.

It's in the Bible!

I have found that everywhere something unusual, extraordinary and out of the ordinary happened in the Bible, somebody had to be willing to do something unusual, extraordinary and out of the ordinary. Check it out for yourself. Extraordinary things didn't just happen. God always brought them to a place where they had to go beyond the norm. They had to do something that they had never done before.

Unfortunately, that's why a lot of Christians are not going to experience the extraordinary; they're not willing to go to the next level. We cannot stay as we are and experience something we've never experienced before.

There is a law that states that every seed produces after its own kind. Genesis 8:22 tells us that as long as the earth remains, seedtime and harvest shall not cease. The earth is still here; we're still living on it, and this law of seedtime and harvest is still governing and controlling our lives. I want the extraordinary in my life every day. I want God to do unusual things in my life every day. I want people to notice and say, "What is it with this guy? Why do these extraordinary things continually happen to him?"

I want it to be obvious that I'm living in the realm of the extraordinary. Remember, we said in the last chapter that one of the reasons God does the extraordinary is to attract others.

We saw in the book of Acts how one extraordinary event in your life could affect a multitude of people. A man who had been crippled all of his life had sat at the gate called Beautiful as a beggar. But when God did the extraordinary, afterwards, Peter preached and many believed. And the believers grew to five thousand. One extraordinary thing affected five thousand other people.

That's why God wants to do the extraordinary in our lives. It's going to be a soul-winning tool, a tool for evangelism. It's going to attract people to God because of what He's doing in your life.

Getting in Position

So how do you get in position to receive? If you want the extraordinary, you have to be willing to do the extraordinary.

We find an example of this in 2 Kings 4:1-2.

Now there cried a certain woman of the wives of the sons of the prophets unto Elisha, saying, Thy servant my husband is dead; and thou knowest that thy servant did fear the Lord: and the creditor is come to take unto him my two sons to be bondmen.

> **And Elisha said unto her, What shall I do for thee? tell me, what hast thou in the house? And she said, Thine handmaid hath not any thing in the house, save a pot of oil.**

Now notice, she didn't have anything but one pot of oil, which was a very small amount.

> **Then he said, Go, borrow thee vessels abroad of all thy neighbours, even empty vessels; borrow not a few. And when thou art come in, thou shalt shut the door upon thee and upon thy sons, and shalt pour out into all those vessels, and thou shalt set aside that which is full.**
>
> **2 Kings 4:2,3**

Here the prophet is asking this woman to do something out of the ordinary. And she needs extraordinary results. After all, when's the last time you were so deep in debt, the creditors were coming for your children? She needed the extraordinary! So she went to God's representative, the prophet Elisha, and asked for help.

He said, "All right, here's what I'm hearing God tell me to tell you. Go to your neighbors and borrow all the empty vessels you can find. Don't borrow just a few."

Don't Shortchange Yourself

This instruction to **borrow not a few** is interesting. God is saying, *Don't shortchange yourself. And don't limit Me.* So when the prophet said, "Don't borrow just a few," he was implying that God didn't want to meet just the need; He wanted to put this woman into the overflow.

So she went to her neighbors' homes. Now, she's doing something out of the norm. How many of us would really do that? We have this word from God: "Go borrow empty vessels. Don't borrow a few. Go to your neighbors, and get all the empty vessels you can."

But you know the neighbors are going to ask, "Why are you doing this? Why do you want these empty jars?"

What are you going to tell them?

"Well, I have a need. I owe some money, and the creditors are going to come and repossess everything I have if I don't pay these bills. So I was praying, and God told me to take the little bottle of oil that I have and go borrow a bunch of empty vessels from my neighbors, and then go to my bedroom and pour the jar of that oil into all the jars that I'm going to borrow from you."

They're going to say, "Not only are you in debt, but you're in need of mental help! I think you've had an emotional breakdown."

This woman is actually doing something that I would call rare. She is about to plant an extraordinary seed that's going to produce extraordinary results. Remember, you're not going to experience the extraordinary if you're not willing to do something that's out of the ordinary.

Notice what happened.

So she went from him, and shut the door upon her and upon her sons, who brought the vessels to her; and she poured out.

And it came to pass, when the vessels were full, that she said unto her son, Bring me yet a vessel. And he said unto her, There is not a vessel more. And the oil stayed.

Then she came and told the man of God. And he said, Go, sell the oil, and pay thy debt, and live thou and thy children of the rest.

2 Kings 4:5-7

By doing something uncommon and rare, this woman not only had an extraordinary manifestation, but it put her into overflow as well.

Not a Single Fish

Let's look at another example from Luke 5.

And it came to pass, that, as the people pressed upon [Jesus] to hear the word of God, he stood by the lake of Gennesaret, and saw two ships standing by the lake: but the fishermen were gone out of them, and were washing their nets. And he entered into one of the ships, which was Simon's, and prayed him that he would thrust out a little from the land. And he sat down, and taught the people out of the ship.

Now when he had left speaking, he said unto Simon, Launch out into the deep, and let down your nets for a draught.

And Simon answering said unto him, Master, we have toiled all the night, and have taken nothing: nevertheless at thy word I will let down the net.

And when they had this done, they inclosed a great multitude of fishes: and their net brake. And they beckoned unto their partners, which were in the other ship, that they should come

**and help them. And they came, and filled both
the ships, so that they began to sink.**

Luke 5:1-7

In this familiar story, these commercial fishermen had
come in one morning empty-handed after they'd been
fishing all night. They had not caught anything after a
night's work. Now that's bad news when you're in the
fishing business. So they were washing their nets. They
were probably tired and discouraged because they did
not have a profitable night. And to top it off, here comes
this preacher who asks Peter, "Let me borrow your boat
while I finish My sermon."

So Jesus got into Peter's boat, pushed away from the
shore, finished His sermon and then turned around to
Peter and said, "Now launch out into the deep and let
down your nets." The Bible says that Peter began to
explain why he couldn't do that. Jesus was asking him to
do something that was out of the ordinary.

Peter said, "Master, we have toiled all night long, and
we've caught nothing." And he almost blew it. He almost
blew his opportunity for the extraordinary, but these
words changed everything: **Nevertheless at Thy word.**
In other words, "You're asking me to do something that is

out of the ordinary. You're asking me to do something that is not in line with the common course of things. You're asking me to do something that is not the norm. I don't feel like it. I don't want to. It doesn't feel right. It doesn't sound right. It doesn't look right, but nevertheless, at Thy word, I'll do it."

Peter did it—and he caught so many fish that his nets began to break. His boat began to sink. He had to beckon to his partners. They came out, and their nets also began to break. Their boats began to sink. Not only did they have an extraordinary catch, but they also got into the overflow.

My point is, in order to receive this rare and uncommon harvest of fish, Peter had to do something that was out of the ordinary. He had to go against his experience as a fisherman and accept the word of Jesus that if he would plant an extraordinary seed, he would reap an extraordinary harvest.

Uncommon Tactics

Throughout the Bible, we continually see God asking people to do extraordinary things so that He can bring extraordinary results into their lives. There is no better example of the extraordinary than the story of what God did for King Jehoshaphat:

> It came to pass after this also, that the children of Moab, and the children of Ammon, and with them other beside the Ammonites, came against Jehoshaphat to battle.
>
> Then there came some that told Jehoshaphat, saying, There cometh a great multitude against thee from beyond the sea on this side Syria; and, behold, they be in Hazazon-tamar, which is Engedi.
>
> And Jehoshaphat feared, and set himself to seek the Lord, and proclaimed a fast throughout all Judah. And Judah gathered themselves together, to ask help of the Lord: even out of all the cities of Judah they came to seek the Lord.
>
> And Jehoshaphat stood in the congregation of Judah and Jerusalem, in the house of the Lord, before the new court, and said, O Lord God of our fathers, art not thou God in heaven? and rulest not thou over all the kingdoms of the heathen? and in thine hand is there not power and might, so that none is able to withstand thee?
>
> Art not thou our God, who didst drive out the inhabitants of this land before thy people Israel,

and gavest it to the seed of Abraham thy friend
for ever? And they dwelt therein, and have built
thee a sanctuary therein for thy name, saying, If,
when evil cometh upon us, as the sword, judg-
ment, or pestilence, or famine, we stand before
this house, and in thy presence, (for thy name is
in this house,) and cry unto thee in our affliction,
then thou wilt hear and help.

And now, behold, the children of Ammon and
Moab and mount Seir, whom thou wouldest not
let Israel invade, when they came out of the land
of Egypt, but they turned from them, and
destroyed them not; behold, I say, how they
reward us, to come to cast us out of thy possession, which thou hast given us to inherit.

O our God, wilt thou not judge them? for we
have no might against this great company that
cometh against us; neither know we what to do:
but our eyes are upon thee.

2 Chronicles 20:1-12

It is no wonder that King Jehoshaphat and his people
were afraid of this huge army that was set to invade their
territory. God's people were totally outnumbered. In the
ordinary course of things, there was no way they could
be victorious in this battle. They didn't have any idea

what to do, so they turned to the Lord for advice. And the Spirit of the Lord instructed Jehoshaphat to do something completely out of the ordinary.

Then upon Jahaziel...a Levite of the sons of Asaph, came the Spirit of the Lord in the midst of the congregation; and he said, Hearken ye, all Judah, and ye inhabitants of Jerusalem, and thou king Jehoshaphat, Thus saith the Lord unto you, Be not afraid nor dismayed by reason of this great multitude; for the battle is not yours, but God's.

Tomorrow go ye down against them: behold, they come up by the cliff of Ziz; and ye shall find them at the end of the brook, before the wilderness of Jeruel. Ye shall not need to fight in this battle: set yourselves, stand ye still, and see the salvation of the Lord with you, O Judah and Jerusalem: fear not, nor be dismayed; tomorrow go out against them: for the Lord will be with you.

And Jehoshaphat bowed his head with his face to the ground: and all Judah and the inhabitants of Jerusalem fell before the Lord, worshipping the Lord.

And the Levites, of the children of the Kohathites, and of the children of the Korhites,

stood up to praise the Lord God of Israel with a loud voice on high. And they rose early in the morning, and went forth into the wilderness of Tekoa: and as they went forth, Jehoshaphat stood and said, Hear me, O Judah, and ye inhabitants of Jerusalem; Believe in the Lord your God, so shall ye be established; believe his prophets, so shall ye prosper.

And when he had consulted with the people, he appointed singers unto the Lord, and that should praise the beauty of holiness, as they went out before the army, and to say, Praise the Lord; for his mercy endureth for ever.

And when they began to sing and to praise, the Lord set ambushments against the children of Ammon, Moab, and mount Seir, which were come against Judah; and they were smitten.

For the children of Ammon and Moab stood up against the inhabitants of mount Seir, utterly to slay and destroy them: and when they had made an end of the inhabitants of Seir, every one helped to destroy another.

And when Judah came toward the watch tower in the wilderness, they looked unto the

multitude, and, behold, they were dead bodies
fallen to the earth, and none escaped.

And when Jehoshaphat and his people came
to take away the spoil of them, they found among
them in abundance both riches with the dead
bodies, and precious jewels, which they stripped
off for themselves, more than they could carry
away: and they were three days in gathering of
the spoil, it was so much.

2 Chronicles 20:14-25

Jehoshaphat told his generals to get all the singers
and put them on the front lines. Now, that is not an ordinary battle tactic. Go read any military manual you can
put your hands on, and it will never tell you that as a last
resort—when everything else fails, your tanks are
destroyed and you've run out of ammunition—go get the
singers and put them on the front line. There's not a military manual in the world that will tell you to do that.

Confounded and Confused

So God was asking them to do something out of the
ordinary—to put the singers on the front lines and have
them praise God and shout, "The Lord is good, and His

mercy endureth forever!" But what was God doing? He was asking them to plant an extraordinary seed. Do something out of the ordinary if you want extraordinary results.

So the Israelites began to praise God, singing and shouting and rejoicing and declaring, "The Lord is good, and His mercy endures forever." The Bible says that it confounded their enemy. Their enemy was confused. And their enemy began to turn on one another. They killed one another until not one of them was left standing.

When God's people stopped singing and shouting, they saw that their enemies were dead. So they gathered up all the spoil. It took them three days to gather up all the gold and silver.

Now, here's something else extraordinary about this story. Why would soldiers carry all their gold and all their silver to war? That's not the norm. Have you ever heard of a soldier carrying all of his gold, silver, stocks, bonds, the title to his car and the deed to his house with him when he is sent to war? No. God had this enemy do something out of the ordinary. Why? Because His people needed it.

This is what God wants to do for you and me. The extraordinary. But it's not going to happen if we are not willing to do something this year that we haven't done before. We won't experience the extraordinary in our finances if we're not willing to sow more than we did last year. It's up to you and me.

Planting for an Uncommon Harvest

The question is this: What do I do to get in position to receive the extraordinary? Every day you need to confess, "God, I'm believing for the extraordinary today, so tell me where to plant an extraordinary seed."

Now you have to have a listening ear. You have to have an ear tuned toward heaven because God's going to speak to you. Let me give you an example. In 1998, my ministry had an opportunity to sow into a project that Kenneth Copeland Ministries was involved in. So I sowed $10,000, and in a few days we received a check from another ministry for $50,000.

The norm is that we take 10 percent of our income, put it in our tithe account, and then we sow it into other ministries. That's the norm. The common. The ordinary. Therefore, when the accounting department showed me the check for $50,000, I said, "Well, you know what to do."

But as I was walking out of our administrative building, going back to my office, I heard this inside of me:

How would you like to see some uncommon results?

I said, "You know I would."

God said, *Then do something uncommon. Plant an uncommon seed.*

I knew exactly what He meant. I went right back to the accounting department and said, "Guys, don't take the tithe from that $50,000 and put it into the tithe account. Today we're going to do something uncommon. We're going to sow the whole $50,000."

And so, in obedience to God, we sowed that entire $50,000. See, that's doing something that is uncommon. And that uncommon seed produced two checks for $100,000 each!

God was trying to show me that the way you bring the extraordinary into your life is by being willing to do something that is uncommon.

Going Beyond

You're going to have to do something that's uncommon in order to get uncommon results. It may be that instead of spending your usual, daily one hour in prayer or your usual, daily one hour in the Word, you'll need to go beyond that this year.

If you have a habit of putting just $25 in the offering plate at church, then go beyond that this year. If nothing else, put in $25.10. Go beyond the norm and watch what God will do for you.

Chapter 4

God's Special Treasure

We have been learning that if we're going to experience the extraordinary, we have to go beyond the norm. We have to break some barriers in our lives. In this chapter, I want to convince you that God truly wants to do extraordinary things in your life simply because you are very special to Him.

What He Did for Paul, He'll Do for You

Let me remind you of what Acts 19:11 says, **And God wrought special miracles by the hands of Paul.** *The*

Amplified Bible translates that verse: **And God did unusual and extraordinary miracles by the hands of Paul.**

Can you believe that *what God did for Paul, He wants to do for you?*

Of course, I realize that Paul was a great man of faith. I realize that Paul holds a very special place in the history of the church. However, if I am reading Paul's writings correctly, one of the things that he emphasized in every letter he wrote was that *we are just as special as he was.* He emphasized that we, too, can expect the same grace, the same favor, the same manifestations as he did. This is one of the distinguishing characteristics of Paul's writings. Everything Paul wrote about had this underlying theme: who we are *in Christ.* That's the reason Paul experienced extraordinary things—he knew who he was in Christ.

And in every letter that he wrote, he endeavored to get it across to all the believers that they, too, were in Christ. In fact, in many of his writings, you'll find that Paul writes about everything that Christ did, and then in the next chapter, he discusses what we can do because we are in Christ.

Jesus expected the extraordinary, and I have reason to believe that Paul expected the extraordinary too. I can't find Jesus saying anywhere in the gospels, "Oh, God, I hope You work through me tonight. Dear God, if You don't do a miracle here at the tomb of Lazarus, they are going to take away my papers." No. He expected God to do the extraordinary anytime it was necessary to meet the needs of humanity.

A Man Approved by God

God did signs and wonders through Jesus because He was a man approved by God. (Acts 2:22.) Do you believe you're approved by God? Do you believe that you have God's stamp of approval on your life? Why shouldn't you—you're just as much God's child as Jesus is.

"Now, wait a minute, Brother Jerry," you might say. "Are you trying to say that I'm equal to Jesus?"

No, I'm not saying that. No one will ever take Jesus' place. He's the King of kings and Lord of lords, but through what He did at Calvary, you and I can stand in God's presence and declare that we are His very own children and that we have right standing with Him just as Jesus does.

Everything that Jesus and Paul experienced—love, grace, mercy, favor—are available to you. You are special to God. One of the major truths Paul emphasized in all of his writings is that you and I have access to everything that he himself had access to. Paul makes that very clear in his letter to the Roman church.

Including You

From the very beginning of the book of Romans, Paul argues that we are special to God and that God does special things for special people.

> **Paul, a servant of Jesus Christ, called to be an apostle, separated unto the gospel of God, (which he had promised afore by his prophets in the holy scriptures,) concerning his Son Jesus Christ our Lord, which was made of the seed of David according to the flesh; and declared to be the Son of God with power, according to the spirit of holiness, by the resurrection from the dead: by whom we have received grace and apostleship, for obedience to the faith among all nations, for**

74

his name: among whom are ye also the called of Jesus Christ.

Romans 1:1-6

The Amplified Bible translates verse 6: **And this includes yourselves, called of Jesus Christ and invited [as you are] to belong to Him.** God has invited me to belong to Him. I am now God's property.

God will never forsake me. God won't forget my name. Why? I'm special to Him. You're special to God. He has invited you to belong to Him. And because we belong to Him, He will do special things for us.

Available to Everyone

Paul said this grace that was on his life has been made available to every member of the body of Christ. He said this includes you and me. Even though he was a great man and even though he holds a very special place in history, he did not walk in any greater favor than what is available to you and me.

Paul reminds us that **God shows no partiality** (Rom. 2:11 AMP). He doesn't care what your race is. He doesn't care what your background is. He doesn't care how much sin you've been involved in once you've asked His forgiveness. He doesn't care how terrible your past has been. God still invites you as you are to belong to Him.

God loves everyone equally. Religion tells us that we're so unworthy. **There is none righteous, no, not one** (Rom. 3:10). Well, that *was* true—until the Cross.

Heaven's Best

Before the Cross, there was none righteous. We deserved to go to a devil's hell. But on the other hand, Romans 5:8 says, **While we were yet sinners, Christ died for us.** So apparently we are of some worth to God, because God gave heaven's best to redeem us.

Don't ever again say, "I'm unworthy." Don't ever say, "I don't deserve that." That's like slapping God in the face and saying the blood of Jesus didn't work, the Cross didn't work, redemption didn't work. I'm not worthy because of what I've done but because of what Jesus did.

God shows no partiality. God's not going down the line saying, "I love thee. I love thee not. I love thee. I love thee not. I'm going to bless thee. But not thee. I like thee, but I'm still trying to determine what I think about thee."

You say, "Well, why are some people more blessed than others?" Because some people have a greater insight into these truths than others. Some people know who they are in Christ. I'm not being egotistical about this. I am simply declaring what the Bible says I am. For me to say anything other than what the Bible says I am would be egotistical, because then I would be accepting only my own opinion about it.

Grasp the Fact

Paul makes it clear that what Jesus did on the cross was done for our sake.

> **That is why** [Abraham's] **faith was accredited to him as righteousness—right standing with God. But [the words], It was accredited to him, were written not for his sake alone, but [they were written] for our sakes too.... Therefore, since we are justified—acquitted, declared right-eous, and given a right standing with God— through faith, let us [grasp the fact that we] have [the peace of reconciliation] to hold and to enjoy,**

**peace with God through our Lord Jesus Christ,
the Messiah, the Anointed One.**

Romans 4:22-24; 5:1 AMP

Now this is where so many members of the body of
Christ miss it. They simply haven't "grasped the fact"
regarding their redemption, and as a result, they're living
way below their privileges as children of God.

You see, if you don't think you're special to God,
you're not going to expect special things. If you think that
you're one of God's stepchildren, then you will say, "Well, I
can understand God doing this for Brother Copeland, but
who am I? I can understand God doing this for Dr. Billy
Graham, but who am I?" If you go around thinking that
you're some kind of second-class citizen, then you're not
going to expect extraordinary things. You'll agree that
they could happen to somebody else but not to you.

However, when you know you're special to God, then
you walk around with your head held high. You walk
around with a smile on your face. You walk around with
a dance in your step, a song in your heart and the Word
of God coming out of your mouth. It won't make any
difference what's happening around you, you just expect
God to turn it around and do something on your behalf.

Why Are We Special to God?

Why does God want to do extraordinary things for us? Because He loves us. God is our Father, and He loves us as His very own children.

I don't think I fully understood how God could love me until I had children of my own. Then I began to discover what a father's love is like. And I really began to understand it when I became a grandfather!

Before then, I couldn't understand why grandparents act so silly over their grandchildren. For example, I remember when we left Shreveport, Louisiana, to move to Texas to work for Brother Copeland. The last thing I saw was my father-in-law, Olen Creech, crying. I mean, he was broken. You would have thought that I had just killed his best hunting dog or something. He was a basket case. The last thing I saw in my rear-view mirror was my father-in-law, standing in his driveway crying because I was taking his granddaughters to Texas.

When we got out on the road, I said to Carolyn, "Did you see your daddy?"

She said, "Yes."

I said, "Why was he crying like that? We're only going two hundred miles away."

She said, "I don't know."

I said, "He acted as though he would never see them again."

I just couldn't understand that—until my daughter JerriAnn decided to move to California with her two boys. Up until then, those two grandsons had lived five minutes from me. And then their mother decided that she's going to California—and taking my grandsons with her!

She'd been wanting to move to California ever since she was in high school. But I'd always talk her out of it.

Finally God said, "You don't have any right to interfere with her dream."

And she said, "Daddy, you've got to let me go."

I said, "Go. Just leave the boys here."

She said, "I can't do that."

So, finally, I agreed to help her move to California. I drove the U-Haul truck, and I had both boys in the front seat with me. I cried for two and a half days. Every time we would stop for fuel or something to eat, Mark James would say, "Mamma, Papa just cries all the time. Why is he crying all the time?" But I couldn't stop. I'd look down at them, and I couldn't stop crying.

It hadn't dawned on them yet that they were actually moving. They knew they were going to California, but it hadn't registered with them yet that they were staying and I was going back to Texas.

When we finally got there, I cried every time I took a piece of furniture out of the truck. I was torn to pieces.

After we got everything moved in, my daughter took me to the hotel near the airport because I was going to fly back early the next morning.

When I got out of the car, Mark James asked, "Papa, where are you going?"

I said, "Well, son, I've got to go back to Texas."

"You're going back to Texas?"

"Yes."

"Am I going with you?"

"No."

"Where am I going, Papa?"

"You're staying here. This is where you live now."

He jumped out of that car and grabbed one of my legs and wrapped his arms around it. He wouldn't let me go. He was crying, "Papa, don't leave us. Don't leave us, Papa!"

Finally, I had to pull him away and put him back in the car. He was crying his little eyes out as his mother drove out of that parking lot. I was such a basket case, I couldn't even find the lobby. The bellman had to take me by the hand and lead me to the front desk.

He said, "Brother Jerry, are you all right?"

I said, "No, I'm not all right."

He had to walk me to the desk and fill out my registration card for me. And then he pointed me to the elevator. There were two elderly men standing there. I couldn't even see the button to push for my floor because I'd cried so much my eyes were nearly swollen shut. So these two elderly men actually walked me to my room and put the key in the door for me.

They said, "Young fellow, you are a mess." And they were right!

How Does God Feel?

Believe me, that was the hardest thing I've ever been through in my life. I mean, I have fought demons all over the world, but I've never been through anything like that.

My point is this: those boys are very special to me. Now, I have two granddaughters, Kassidi and Madison, and they are very special to me as well. And you know I love each of them the same. I'm no respecter of grand-children, you could say.

Well, just think of the love of God. How many times do you suppose God has wept over us when He's trying to bless us but we won't let Him—when He's trying to deliver us but we won't let Him, when He is trying to get to us everything that He said belongs to us in our covenant but we won't let Him. That has to be heart-breaking to God.

God loves us so much that He made us His heirs:

The Spirit itself beareth witness with our spirit, that we are the children of God: and if children, then heirs; heirs of God, and joint-heirs with Christ.

Romans 8:16,17

The Bible points out that our position in Christ is important. You need to get a revelation of who you are in Christ and never let anyone take it away from you.

You're an heir of God and a joint heir with Jesus Christ. It's the devil who tries to make you feel that you're not special. It's religion that makes you feel that you're not worthy.

"You Won't Do"

I remember one time when I was working for Brother Copeland, we were in Kansas City at a Full Gospel Businessmen's convention. It was about 1973. And as it turned out, the hotel fouled up on our reservations, and there was only one room with two beds; so Brother Copeland and I had to stay in the same room together, which we normally didn't do. This was the first time I'd ever stayed in the same room with him while we were in a meeting.

After he preached that night, we went back to our room, and Brother Copeland went to bed. But I stayed up reading with a small lamp on so I wouldn't disturb him. It was after midnight, and Brother Copeland was sound asleep.

Suddenly, there was a knock on the door. So I went to see who it was. There was a man at the door and he said, "I need to see Kenneth Copeland."

I closed the door just enough so our conversation wouldn't disturb Brother Copeland. I said, "Well, sir, Brother Copeland's asleep. You can't see him now."

He said, "It's important. I need to see him right now. I've got something I've got to tell him."

I said, "Well, sir, he's asleep. He went to bed right after he got through preaching tonight. Were you in the meeting?"

"Yes, I was in the meeting. That's what I need to see him about."

I said, "I'm his Associate Minister. This is what I'm here for. Tell me what you need, and I'll be glad to help you."

But he said, "No, you won't do."

"Well, sir," I said, "you can't see Brother Copeland. I'm sorry, but you just can't see him. He's asleep."

He said, "Then wake him up."

I said, "No, I'm not going to wake him up."

Then he got louder and more belligerent. But I said, "Sir, do you understand? I'm his associate. This is my job. I will be happy to help you. I'll get dressed. I'll go downstairs with you. I'll counsel you, minister to you, and pray with you. And if I don't know the answer to your questions, I promise you that when Brother Copeland wakes up in the morning, I'll ask him. I'll look for you and give you his answer."

But he said again, "No, you won't do."

And then he shoved me so hard that I fell against the door and wound up on the floor. Well, that woke Brother Copeland up—just before I was about to sin. So I jumped off that floor with every intention of doing my best to deck this man.

But Brother Copeland got up, thank God, and then he walked over to the man and said, "Did you hear what Jerry said?"

I didn't know Brother Copeland had heard our conversation. He asked the man again, "Did you hear what Jerry said?"

The man said, "Yes, but I need to talk to you."

Brother Copeland spoke very bluntly to him about how wrong he was and asked him to leave. The man walked off, and Brother Copeland went back to bed.

A Wounded Spirit

I went back to bed, too, but as I lay there, I kept thinking about this incident. And the only phrase that I could remember was, *You won't do.* It reminded me of another time when I was a young boy and somebody told me that I wouldn't do. These words can wound your spirit. So I'm lying there in bed, hearing those words: *You won't do. You won't do.* In other words, the man meant that I wasn't good enough. I wasn't anointed enough.

Words like that don't make you feel very special. And once you start entertaining thoughts like that, the devil will work overtime. Boy, he loves it. He thinks, *Oh, I've got him now. He's thinking he's not good enough. He thinks he's not smart enough. He thinks he's not qualified.*

It also reminds me of something that happened to me when I was a young boy. It was while I was trying out for my first little league baseball team. My best friend and I tried out for the team, and when it came time to select those who were going to make the team, the coach told me that I couldn't play because I was too little. In other words, "You won't do."

He said, "I'm sorry, but you're just too little."

It broke my heart. I knew I could play baseball as well as anybody else. But he said I was too little. Later that day my mother came to get me and my best friend, Kenny, who had also tried out for the team. Kenny was selected. He was bigger than I was. We were the same age, but he was always bigger. I was sitting in the front seat and Kenny was in the backseat. I was doing everything I could do to keep from crying, because what that coach had said to me wounded my spirit. I had my heart set on playing baseball.

I was just sitting there not saying a word. Suddenly, Kenny said, "Did you tell your mother you didn't make the team because you're too little?" When he said that, it literally broke my heart. I cried and cried and cried. I can remember it just like it was yesterday.

When we arrived home, I sat in my room and continued to cry. I felt as though I wasn't normal because I was so little, and I hated being little.

Two Vows

However, because of that experience, I remember making two vows: I vowed that I'd never cry again and that I would prove that I was as good and as big as all the other boys.

Of course, I wasn't looking forward to going to school the next morning. I knew I'd have to face the boys who knew I hadn't made the team because the coach said that I was too little. But when I got to school, they announced that since there were so many boys who had tried out for the team, they decided to start another team and invite all the boys who didn't make the first team to try out for the second one.

I said, "I'm going and I will make this team."

And I did make the team! Not only that, but those two teams ended up being in the playoffs and our team won, and I was the winning pitcher!

The next year, the coach who had told me that I was too little came to our house and asked my dad if I could play on his team. I overheard the conversation.

When I came into the room, I said, "No sir, I can't play for your team because I'm too little."

I never played for his team, and our team beat his team every year. Later, several teams in our town invited me to play for them.

Sincerely Wrong

I believe what happened to me as a little boy has happened to many Christians. A sincere but sincerely wrong religious person may have told you that you're unworthy and that God doesn't love you. They might have told you that you're just a worm and a dog in His sight. And if that gets down in your spirit then it can wound you.

That's the reason Paul said, "When you grasp the fact...." In other words, when you get a revelation of who you are in Christ, then you're going to realize that God is no respecter of persons. You'll begin to realize that if God will bless anyone, then *He will do it for you as well.*

Handpicked by God

How can you truly know that you're entitled to God's blessings? Because, according to the apostle Paul, God has chosen you.

God's Special Treasure

> **Blessed be the God and Father of our Lord
> Jesus Christ, who hath blessed us with all spiri-
> tual blessings in heavenly places in Christ:
> according as he hath chosen us in him before the
> foundation of the world.**
>
> Ephesians 1:3,4

The Amplified Bible says God **actually picked us out
for Himself as His own** (Eph. 1:4). Have you ever heard
the phrase, "the elect of God"? Paul often talks about the
elect of God. In the literal Greek, the word *elect* means
"picked out."[1] You are handpicked by God. Every time I
read that phrase, it reminds me of the incident that I told
you about in chapter 1, in which Kenneth Copeland
singled me out in the middle of his sermon and told me
that he and I would become a team.

You have been chosen. You have been set apart.
You have been handpicked. God has included you.
**Therefore, you are no longer outsiders—exiles,
migrants and aliens, excluded from the rights of
citizens; but you now share citizenship with the
saints—God's own people, consecrated and set
apart for Himself; and you belong to God's [own]
household** (Eph. 2:19 AMP).

91

A Peculiar People

Peter also realized that when you are in Christ, you are very special to God.

But ye are a chosen generation, a royal priesthood, an holy nation, a peculiar people.

1 Peter 2:9

The word *peculiar* does not mean "weird." It means "God's own possession."[2]

Therefore, the next time you hear the devil—or anyone else—telling you that "you won't do," remind him that you are a peculiar person. You're set apart; you're chosen. You're included. You're handpicked. You're God's own possession. You're God's special treasure. You've been made righteous. You're worthy. You are one of God's greatest creations.

Chapter 5

The Importance of Expectancy

God wants to do the extraordinary for every one of us. However, as we have seen, often He can't because we fail to get in a position to receive.

So far, we've discussed several ways in which we can cooperate with God in bringing the extraordinary into our lives. We've said that we must go beyond the norm, and we must break some barriers in our lives. Also, we must stop thinking of ourselves as unworthy of God's attention, and we must begin to see ourselves as the Bible sees us—as God's special people.

Now I want to look at another important factor in our getting in position to receive the extraordinary: The importance of keeping our expectations high. Expectancy is vital, because the more you expect the extraordinary, the more you will see it.

"Something Told Me..."

God wants us to begin to expect the extraordinary in our finances. That's why I have written this book: I want you to begin to expect things to happen to you financially that are out of the ordinary.

I want you to begin expecting to hear this phrase from other people often: *"Something told me...."*

For instance, at one of the churches where I was preaching this message, I told the congregation on a Friday night to expect to hear this phrase. Before the service the next night, the pastor told me that earlier in the day, a lady who had been driving by the church suddenly pulled into the parking lot and came into the church bookstore. She was crying. The people in the bookstore thought she was in some kind of trouble. However she said, "*Something* told me to bring this money here and I've never even been to this church before." The pastor said, "We've never had anything like that happen to us before."

Remember what I said in the last chapter: *What God has done for others, He will do for you if you will only believe and expect Him to do it.*

Expectation Is Not Based on Fantasy

Critics of "faith preachers" have accused us of building up people's hopes. But we're not basing this expectation on some kind of fantasy. Our hope is based on the Word of God. The Bible is a book of hope. It's the God of hope whom we serve. Psalm 62:5 says, **My soul, wait thou only upon God; for my expectation is from him.**

I'm not endeavoring to build your hopes on fantasies. I'm endeavoring to build your hopes on "Thus saith the Lord." The Bible says, **Believe in the Lord your God, so shall ye be established; believe his prophets, so shall ye prosper** (2 Chron. 20:20).

Well, if you truly believe God, that will create expectation in your spirit.

You can't truly believe God and expect nothing. You can't say "I'm living by faith" without expecting something to happen. When you live by faith, you expect the miraculous all the time. You may not know how God's going to do it, but you still expect Him to come through for you. I never know how God's going to do it. In fact, I quit trying to figure that out years ago! It's not my job to try to figure out how God's going to do something. It's my job to believe He will, to expect it and to thank Him for it.

I don't know about you, but I love surprises. God can just surprise me any way that He wants. He can surprise me every day. I love surprises. It still amazes me how God can bless me in ways that I would never have dreamed possible. Let me tell you a story about one of the ways God surprised me with a blessing.

All the Way From Boston

A few years ago, Brother Jesse Duplantis and I were preaching together in Augusta, Georgia. We arrived there the day before the meeting started. Jesse and his wife,

Cathy, and my wife, Carolyn, and I went out for a walk around the city and were just having a good time together.

As we started back toward the hotel, a young girl about nine or ten years old came running toward me, shouting, "Brother Jerry, Brother Jerry!"

I didn't know who she was. I'd never seen her before, but when I got near her, she just grabbed me, threw her arms around me and said, "Oh, Brother Jerry, God told me that I would run into you. I prayed that I would see you."

I said, "Is that right?"

She said, "Yes, my mother and my sisters and brothers and I came to this meeting to hear you and Brother Jesse. We drove all the way from Boston, Massachusetts."

She explained that they had driven all that way in an old car that I'm certain only got there because of their faith! It looked like the one I used to own when I went to work for Brother Copeland back in 1990. They believed God that it was going to make it all the way to Georgia so they could be in that meeting.

The car quit running right in front of the hotel where Jesse and I were staying. They had received the announcement about the meeting and saw that this hotel was one that we had recommended.

However, they didn't have any money to stay in this hotel or any other hotel. They just drove there to ask someone how to get to the auditorium where the meeting was being held.

This woman had all those children in that car, and I think that they had planned to sleep in it.

But the car quit on them right in front of the hotel, and the mother couldn't get it started again. She laid her head on the steering wheel and cried, and her little girl said, "Well, Mamma, I'll just pray that God will send Brother Jerry. He used to work on cars. He will help us."

She got out of the car and started walking through the parking lot and saw me coming toward her. That's when she started running and shouting, "Brother Jerry, Brother Jerry!"

So I said, "Well, how can I help you?"

She said, "My mother's car has quit. It won't start. And she's crying, and we don't know what to do. So I prayed that God would send you to us."

I walked over to where the lady was. She still had her head on the steering wheel, and she was crying. I put my hand on her shoulder and said, "Ma'am, can I help you?"

She looked up and exclaimed, "My God, it's Jerry Savelle!"

And the little girl said, "I told you, Mamma."

I said, "What seems to be the problem?"

She said, "My car won't start." Then she told me the whole story about how God had gotten them to Georgia.

I said, "Well, Ma'am, there's nothing I can do, but I'll get one of my associates to call a tow truck and we'll have it towed to a garage. We'll get it repaired, and I'll pay for it."

"You're Not Getting All the Blessing!"

Well, Jesse was standing there hearing all of this. And when I said, "Don't worry—I'll pay for it," Jesse said, "Just a minute—you're not getting all that blessing."

I said, "What do you mean?"

He said, "I'm paying for half of this."

"Well, if that's what you want to do," I said.

So we arranged to have a tow truck take the car to a garage to be repaired.

Then I asked, "Where are you folks staying?"

They said, "We were going to stay in the car."

I said, "Well, you can't stay in the car. You'll have to stay in a hotel."

They said, "But we don't have any money to stay in a hotel."

I said, "Well, anybody who will drive all the way from Boston, Massachusetts, to hear Jesse and me preach is going to stay in a hotel. I'll get you a room, and I'll pay for it."

I told the children, "They've got a menu in the room. You just order whatever you want to eat. I'll pay for it."

Jesse said, "You're not getting all that blessing. I'm paying for half of this."

So we got them a room. And the opening night of the meeting, the little girl ran up to me and said, "Brother Jerry, did you know that they have people at that hotel who carry your bags up to the room for you? They would not even let us carry our own bags!"

.

She was so excited because it was the first time she'd
ever been in a hotel. They were having a wonderful time.
Well, we got their car repaired, and Jesse and I paid for it.
We paid for their room, and we loaded them up with
tapes and books and gave them some money to get back
home. They wrote to us later and shared their testimony
about what a blessing it was to the entire family.

All a Seed Knows To Do

Now, what I want you to see in this story is this: A
seed only knows how to do one thing—produce a
harvest. To ask a seed not to produce is to violate spiritual law. I didn't say out loud, "I'm believing for a return
on this seed." Neither one of us was thinking that when
we decided to help this family. We just did it because we
wanted to. We wanted to bless them.

The Harvest Always Comes

Well, about two weeks later, I was preaching in my
monthly rally at my ministry headquarters in Fort Worth,
Texas. I said to the people at the end of the service,
"Forgive me; I'm not going to be able to stay around to

visit and shake hands with you. I've got a call that I have
to make immediately after this service to my International
Director in Kenya. We have some serious business to
discuss, and he's expecting me to call him. It's eight
hours later there, and I have to call him as soon as I get
out of this meeting. I'm going to have one of my associates pray and dismiss you, and I'm going to slip out so I
can make that call."

When I got through preaching, I had one of my associates come up to pray. I took my Bible and my Bible case,
and I walked down through the middle aisle to go out
the back door of the auditorium. As I was walking out, a
man stopped me in the aisle, put something in my hand
and said quietly, "Read this and give me a call."

I said, "Okay," and I slipped the note in the pocket of
my Bible case.

By the time I had made my call and taken care of my
business, it was nearly midnight. My wife was out of
town, so it was one of those rare times when I was home
alone. It was late, so I went to bed and forgot to read that
note. It wasn't until the next morning when I was having
my breakfast that I remembered it.

The Importance of Expectancy

So I went to my study, got the note out of my Bible case and sat down to read it. The note said, "I know you like Chevrolet Corvettes. I'd like to provide one for you. Call me if you're interested."

Well, it was 7 a.m. I thought, *I wonder if he's awake yet. I better wait a few minutes before I call.* So I waited until 7:12 and called the number on the note.

I said, "Are you awake?"

He said, "I've been waiting on you. What took you so long? I expected you to call last night."

I said, "I forgot to read your note last night."

He said, "Well, I live in Dallas, and I'm one of your partners. I know you like Corvettes. Do you have one right now?"

I said, "As a matter of fact, I have a 1961 model that I'm restoring, but I sold my late-model one last year."

He said, "Well, are you interested in a new one?"

I said, "Yes, sir!"

He said, "Well, when can you come?"

I said, "It normally takes about an hour to drive to Dallas from here, but I can be there in about thirty minutes!"

"Okay," he said, "meet me at the dealership. I want you to select one, and let's see if you pick the same one that I did."

So I went to Dallas and met him at the dealership. The showroom was full of Corvettes, with every color that they made that year. I found the one I liked and said, "This is it."

He said, "That's the very one that I picked out."

A Call From Jesse

After arranging to have the car that I had driven there driven back to Fort Worth, I drove my new Corvette home. Shortly after I got home, the telephone rang. It was Jesse Duplantis. Jesse said, "Hey! Has anything unusual happened to you in the last twenty-four hours?"

I said, "Why?"

He said, "Man, something out of the ordinary has happened to me, and I think it has something to do with that seed we planted in those people in Augusta, Georgia. Did you ask God for a return on that seed?"

I said, "No. I hadn't even thought about it."

Brother Jesse said, "I didn't either. But God did something for me last night. It was big. It was wonderful, and I thought I'd just call to see if He'd done something unusual for you."

I said, "Yes, He has. But I'm not going to tell you what He did. You're going to have to come and see for yourself."

So in a few days he and Cathy came to Fort Worth to visit us and see my blessing!

Seeds Don't Know Any Better

Jesse and I rejoiced over each other's harvest. Later I asked the Lord why we he had done these unusual things for us.

He answered, *Son, the last thing I told seeds to do when I made them was to produce a harvest. Therefore, they don't know any better. All a seed knows to do is grow. A seed will do its best to grow when it's planted. Even if you throw it out in the middle of the highway, it*

will do its best to spring up. It may not be in the right soil,
but it will do its best, because that's all it knows to do.

God Wants You To Have Things

If you put God first, if you show Him that He's first
place in your life, then things are going to begin to be
added to your life like never before. God's not against
you having things. He's against things having you. Would
you truly like to know how you can tell if things have
you? If you can't give them away when God asks you to,
then you don't have them; they have you.

I've ridden motorcycles almost my whole life. I started
riding on the back of a Harley-Davidson with my dad
when I was about seven years old, and I've been riding
them ever since. I love riding motorcycles. Brother
Copeland and I have been riding together for nearly
twenty years.

When I went into the ministry in 1969, I gave up my
motorcycle riding. I didn't care if I ever rode another
one. However, after I'd been in the ministry for about
twelve years, God started blessing me with motorcycles

again. In fact, a man gave me a brand-new one. He said God told him to do it.

I said, "Are you sure about this?"

He said, "Yes, I am."

I said, "Why would God tell you to give me a motorcycle since I gave them up when I went into the ministry?"

He said, "Well, I don't know, but I believe I can hear God as well as you can."

So I said, "Well, I believe you can, so I receive it in Jesus' name."

Then I asked the Lord, "Why did You do this? I didn't ask You for a motorcycle."

He answered, *I'm blessing you with it because now I know that I'm first place in your life.*

Several years later, I had two brand-new Harley-Davidsons that I'd been blessed with. Both of them had fewer than 500 miles on them. One was an Ultra Classic® Electra Glide touring bike, and the other was a Heritage Softail Classic. Both of them were gorgeous.

One day I got on my Heritage and started riding out in the countryside, when all of a sudden, I felt like I was riding somebody else's motorcycle. I just knew that this was not my bike anymore.

When I got home, I began to pray and I said, "Lord, these are just toys to me. You have blessed me with these motorcycles so I could enjoy them, but I believe there is somebody who has a ministry that depends on a Harley-Davidson to fulfill what You have called him to do."

God is raising up all kinds of ministries. There are ministers now who are reaching out to outlaw bikers. And they can't do it without a motorcycle, and preferably a Harley, because that's what most of the outlaw bikers are riding.

So I said, "God, I know You have someone out there who ministers to outlaw bikers, and for them this motor-cycle wouldn't be a toy; it would be a tool. Show me where he is, and I'm going to turn my toy into a tool."

As it turned out, this man was one of the students in my Bible school. In fact, he was just about to graduate. Prior to coming to my school he'd been in prison. This man had been so mean that they had to keep him locked away by himself most of the time. But his wife kept believing God for him. Eventually he was saved and baptized in the Holy Ghost. He also accepted the call to preach, and God supernaturally got him out of prison.

He enrolled in my Bible school, and his life had been changed tremendously. His real name was Richard Morgan, but everyone calls him Bear. God said, *There's your man.* So I gave him the Heritage Classic. Later I gave the other motorcycle to another ministry that also reached out to outlaw bikers.

Its First Convert

Before I gave that Harley to Bear, I laid my hands on it and commanded it to be a tool for preaching the Gospel and winning people to Jesus. And do you know, that very afternoon Bear and his wife rode that Harley to the grocery store. He sat out in the parking lot while she went inside. Well, a man walked up to him and said, "Mister, that's got to be one of the most beautiful motorcycles that I've ever seen."

Bear said, "Come here; I want to tell you how I got it."

Now, you don't walk away when Bear wants to witness to you. You don't walk away when Bear says, "I want to talk to you about Jesus." Even if you don't want to hear about Jesus, you'll listen. So the man came over and Bear began to talk to him about the Lord and how we had just given him that motorcycle.

Bear said, "I want you to know that I was in prison for over twenty years, but God delivered me." He went on to say, "And now I'm in Bible school. I've been praying for a motorcycle because I've been ministering to outlaw bikers, and God gave me this motorcycle."

Then Bear asked the man, "Are you saved?"

And he said, "Well, I used to be."

"What do you mean, you used to be?"

"Well, I was but I'm not really serving the Lord now."

Bear said, "Bow your head. We're going to pray."

And right there in that parking lot, Bear led this man back to the Lord. In less than a few hours after I had laid my hands on that motorcycle and commanded it to be a tool for preaching the Gospel through Bear's ministry, that Harley-Davidson had attracted its first convert!

The End of the Story

Now, Bear had no idea that he'd be sitting in class one day, and before he left, he would own a brand-new motorcycle. See, people think God can't do things like this. Or perhaps they think He can, but just not for them. They shake their heads and say, "I just don't believe God could do that for me." But He can and He will, if you'll trust Him and begin to expect it. Most Christians have no idea how special they are to God.

What God's looking for today are people who will serve Him faithfully. No matter what may happen, they will faithfully serve Him. That's the attitude God is looking for. And when He finds people with this kind of attitude, He loads them with blessings. He adds things to their lives so that their lives will become attractive to others. Then they can tell them about their God and how much He loves them and wants to supply their every need.

When I gave these bikes away, as far as I was concerned, I didn't care if I ever rode another motorcycle in my life. But, of course, that was not the end of the story.

"He's Thinking About It"

One day my grandson Mark James and I were driving to the mall in my car when he said, "Papa, is Jesus going to give us another Harley?"

I said, "Well, I don't know, son. I haven't asked Him. Have you?"

He said, "Yes." (He loves to ride motorcycles with me.)

"You asked Jesus to give us another motorcycle?"

"Yes."

So I asked, "Well, what did He say?" I'll never forget his answer as long as I live.

He looked over at me and said, "Papa, Jesus is just like you; He's thinking about it."

I said, "What do you mean by that?"

He said, "Well, Papa, sometimes when I ask you for something, you tell me, 'I'll think about it.'"

I said, "What happens when I think about it?"

He said, "I usually get it. And that's what Jesus is doing right now. He's thinking about it."

So I said, "Then that means we're going to get another one."

He said, "Yes, we will, Papa."

Later I shared this with Brother Jesse and he said, "*Jerry, for you to ask a seed not to produce is a violation of spiritual law.*"

And do you know what happened? God gave me several motorcycles! My cup runneth over!

Stay Expectant

What God wants to know is simply this: Do you believe He can do what you need Him to do? Do you believe He will? If so, then God wants you to stay expectant. That's what the psalmist said.

> **My soul, wait thou only upon God; for my expectation is from him. He only is my rock and my salvation: he is my defence; I shall not be moved. In God is my salvation and my glory: the rock of my strength, and my refuge, is in God. Trust in him at all times.**
>
> **Psalm 62:5-8**

Expect the Extraordinary

We should be saying what the psalmist said: "I have an expectation in my heart that came from God, and I cannot be moved." I've always lived expectantly, but my expectancy has gone to another level, particularly where the extraordinary is concerned. I got this expectancy from God. My expectation is from Him. Recently, He told me that what once was rare is going to become the norm.

I believe this revelation is for every member of the body of Christ. Go through the day talking about it. Go to bed with it on your mind. Begin to declare: "This is my year for the extraordinary, and I'm expecting it every day of my life."

Chapter 6

Fearless Confidence

One of the best ways to keep your expectations high is to remember that God promises to reward your faith.

Sometimes people are afraid to raise their expectations because they don't want to be disappointed if God doesn't come through. But I don't know the God who doesn't come through. I know the God who does.

Before I surrendered my life to God, I used to hear people say, "Don't get your hopes up too high. You never know what God might do." Well, if you read the Bible, you do. God is a God of integrity. I have discovered that God does exactly what He says He'll do in His Word. *How* He is going to do it I don't know. But this one thing I do know; He does what He says He will do.

A person came to me one time and said, "How can you be so confident when you never know what God's going to do?"

I said, "I always know what God's going to do. It's people I can't figure out."

I never know what people are going to do, but I know what God's going to do. He is faithful.

> **Let not thine heart envy sinners: but be thou in the fear of the Lord all the day long.**
>
> **For surely there is an end; and thine expectation shall not be cut off.**
>
> **Proverbs 23:17,18**

When the Bible says your **expectation shall not be cut off,** it means that you will not be disappointed. *The Amplified Bible* says, **For surely there is a latter end [a future and a reward]; and your hope and expectation shall not be cut off** (Prov. 23:18 AMP). What's God saying? He is saying, *I will reward you for your faith; your* *expectations will not be cut off. You are not going to be disappointed. You're going to get exactly what you expect.*

Expectancy Made the Difference

Have you ever wondered why there are so many people healed at Benny Hinn's meetings? Because the people come into his meetings expecting something to happen. Why did so many miracles happen in Kathryn Kuhlman's meetings? Because people came through the door expecting to receive. They heard about the miracles, and they felt that if they could just get into that building, they could be touched by the power of the Holy Spirit.

Actually, there are many sinners who got healed in those meetings. A lot of people who have never made Jesus Lord of their lives got healed and delivered. And there are Christians there who didn't get healed. Why? Their expectancy. Some came not expecting to get anything, and others came expecting to be touched by God's power. And both got what they expected. The ones who expected nothing got nothing. The ones who expected to be healed got healed.

That's the reason people pack out those arenas. They walk into the place expecting the miraculous. And since the Bible says that our expectancy will not be cut off, then they see the miraculous. Their expectations put them in position to receive.

There is a reward for your expectations. You're going to get exactly what you expect, good or bad, negative or positive. So since you're going to get what you expect, then it's to your advantage to expect the best. However, we must realize that just because God says He will not disappoint you, that doesn't mean the reward will always come instantly. Sometimes it does, but usually you must be willing to stand in faith before the extraordinary manifests. Believing for the extraordinary requires patience and perseverance.

Expecting a Payday

The New Testament teaches us to expect a reward. Hebrews 10:35 warns, **Cast not away therefore your confidence which hath great recompense of reward.** *The Amplified Bible* says, **Do not, therefore, fling away your fearless confidence, for it carries a**

great and glorious compensation of reward. Notice the word *compensation*. When I see the word *compensation*, I think "payday."

What's God saying? Simply this, "Don't let go of your expectations. Don't let go of your faith. Stay focused."

Why? Because there is a great recompense of reward. There is a compensation. Payday is coming.

Everybody who has a job expects to get paid. You know when it's payday. Nobody forgets it's payday. And something happens on payday. You have expectancy. You're expecting to be rewarded for the labor you've done during the last week.

When I first went to work for Brother Copeland in 1970, one of the first things he said to me was this: "Jerry, I know you're supposed to be here. God told me that you are, but in the natural I can't afford you. And if you ever get paid, it'll be because you use your faith." Those were his opening remarks my first day on the job.

Well, my family got settled in, and then I was scheduled to go with Brother Copeland for several weeks. All I had was three dollars. I gave those three dollars to my wife. I was going to be away for three weeks. You can't live on three dollars for three weeks, not even in 1970. Carolyn went to church that night and put those three dollars in the offering. She said, "Well, since this won't meet my need, it's now seed." And God took care of her the whole three weeks that I was away.

I remember the first two weeks that I was away and we were supposed to get paid back home. One evening, Brother Copeland called my room and said, "Have you been using your faith?"

I said, "Yes, sir."

He said, "I told you that if you ever got paid it will be because you used your faith. I just called back home and they told me that after all the bills were paid, there wasn't any left for payroll. Are you sure that you have been using your faith?"

I said, "Yes, sir." And then I began to pray. I needed my money. My wife and children needed that money.

A Point of Contact

There I was in that little motel in Portsmouth, Virginia. I hung the phone up after talking to Brother Copeland

and that little room became my wailing wall. I mean, I started praying. I was shouting at the devil and praying in tongues. I knew other people could hear me. I didn't care if they did—I needed my money! I was binding everything that could be bound, and when I couldn't think of anything else to bind, I loosed everything that could be loosed. I did everything I knew to do from Genesis to Revelation. I needed my money!

Later, we went to the evening meeting. I drove Brother Copeland to the meeting. Back then you didn't talk to him unless he started the conversation. So I just drove, and nothing else was said about payday. We went to the meeting, and when it was over, I drove him back to the motel. He still never said anything until we got to his room. That's when he told me that the money had come in right after he had talked to me on the phone. He didn't tell me because he had heard me praying and decided, "Don't tell Jerry that we got paid, because the way he's praying he'll believe in next month's payroll too."

Praise God, I was not disappointed. God came through then, and He's been coming through for me ever since that time.

Don't Wait Until You Get to Heaven

As I've already said, when payday comes around, you expect to get paid. God essentially says in Hebrews 10:35, "Don't cast away your confidence, for there's a payday coming." However, you might be asking, "But *when* are we going to get paid? Is it when we get to heaven?" Now, I realize that there *are* some rewards for us when we get to heaven. But we have been putting too much off until heaven that we could have down here. God wants us to have a payday down here on earth. Remember, Hebrews 10:35 says that there is a great recompense of reward. Now look at what Proverbs 11:31 says, **Behold, the righteous shall be recompensed in the earth.**

Well, are we still on the earth? I assume that you're not reading this book on another planet somewhere. God says that there is a payday coming to the righteous while they're *still on the earth.*

Folks, Jesus' appearing is soon. We are the generation that's going to usher in King Jesus! And if His appearing is soon, then payday must be sooner than that, because the righteous will be recompensed on the earth.

The Law of Increase

There is that scattereth, and yet increaseth; and there is that withholdeth more than is meet, but it tendeth to poverty. The liberal soul shall be made fat: and he that watereth shall be watered also himself.

Proverbs 11:24,25

Here the Bible is saying that the person who is a sower, a giver, is going to be blessed. They're going to abound, and they're going to increase financially. When? Verse 31 says **in the earth.** Hallelujah! I don't have to wait until I get to heaven. Actually, I'm not going to need it in heaven. I need it down here!

The Bible says in Proverbs 13:22, **The wealth of the sinner is laid up for the just.** *The Amplified Bible* says, **The wealth of the sinner [finds its way eventually] into the hands of the righteous, for whom it was laid up.** Well, when is eventually? In heaven? No. What are we going to do with the wealth of the sinner in heaven? What in the world will you spend it on in heaven?

Yes, there are rewards in heaven. There is a crown for the soul winner in heaven. But the wealth transfer has to take place in the earth. Time is running out. I believe it has begun, and that's the reason God wants us to raise our expectations—because the recompense that belongs to the righteous is upon us.

The God of Recompense

The prophet Jeremiah says clearly that God is a God of recompense.

> **Because the spoiler is come upon her, even upon Babylon, and her mighty men are taken, every one of their bows is broken: for the Lord God of recompences shall surely requite.**
>
> **Jeremiah 51:56**

Now, I don't use the word *requite* in my everyday language, so I looked it up in my Webster's Dictionary to see what it means. And it means "to retaliate."[1]

Here's what the Spirit of God said to me when I read that verse. He said, *Son, I am the God of recompense.* That means there is a payday coming for the righteous and a payback coming to the adversary. Did you know the Bible says that God laughs at His enemies because He knows His day is coming? (Psa. 37:13.)

God is the God of recompense. That means that He's going to reward you for your faithfulness. And He's going to pay back your adversary for ever attacking you, putting you under pressure and causing you to have sleepless nights. For every time you've wondered, *What in the world are we going to do? How are we ever going to get out of this mess?* God says, *I'm going to reward you for your faithfulness, and I'm going to pay back your adversary for ever launching an attack on you.* I want you to know that Satan is in serious trouble!

You might say, "Well, how is He going to pay Satan back?" He's going to go to his reservoirs and take the wealth that the wicked have hoarded up and put it in the hands of the righteous so He can reward them for their faithfulness.

Satan has been attacking God's people financially for years; he's been hoarding up the wealth that rightfully belongs to them, trying to keep it out of their hands. But God promises that there is a recompense for the righteous in the earth. They're going to be paid. They're going to be rewarded. They're going to be compensated. They're going to get what's coming to them. It's theirs. It belongs to them. It's their portion. And where's God going to get it? He's going to retaliate against Satan. He's going to take it out of the devil's reservoirs and put it in the body of Christ, where it rightfully belongs.

Don't you think that's going to strike a nerve with the devil? The love of money is the root of all evil. That's what he loves more than anything else. Well, God will strike him at the core and take away what he loves the most.

Payday's coming to you and me, and payback's coming to the devil. Don't give up now. It's reward time. Stay focused and stay expectant. This is the moment you've been waiting for.

Chapter 7

Giving God Something To Work With

Throughout this book, I've stated that if we are going to see the extraordinary manifested in our lives, we must begin to expect it and stand in faith for it. If you want the rare, the unusual and the extraordinary to happen in your life, then you must determine that it's God's will, and you must expect it to happen every day of your life.

When the Spirit of God told me on December 11, 1998, that extraordinary things would become the norm in my life, I became consumed with that possibility. I preached it everywhere I went. My message in every meeting and in every conference that I was invited to throughout the first part of 1999 was this: Expect the Extraordinary.

Another Day for the Extraordinary

Consequently, my thoughts were on this subject continually. I thought about it day and night. I got up in the morning declaring, "This is another day that God will do extraordinary things in my life." I'd go to bed thinking, *Tomorrow is going to be another day for extraordinary things.* Every sermon, every city, every church, every convention—wherever I went—I preached about it.

And during the first five months of 1999, I was getting exactly what I preached. I got exactly what I declared by faith. Extraordinary things were happening to me and around me everywhere I went!

"That's Your Fault!"

However, as I got into the early part of the summer of that year, I noticed that I was not having as many extraordinary events take place in my life as I had during the first part of the year. So I asked the Lord about it.

I asked, "Lord, why am I not experiencing as many uncommon things, special things or unusual things as I did during the first quarter? You said that 1999 would be an extraordinary year. You didn't say it would end after the first quarter."

He said, *That's your fault.*

Now, that's not what I wanted to hear. I wanted it to be somebody else's fault, or I wanted it to be some deep revelation that no one has ever heard of before.

It was like the time many years ago when Brother Copeland said to me, "I told you what your problem is— it's your big mouth." That's not what I wanted to hear back then. I wanted it to be a deep revelation. Unfortunately, it doesn't get much deeper than "your big mouth."

An Arresting Phrase

So, I began praying about why there had been a reduction in the number of extraordinary events, and God led me to Romans 13:14.

**But put ye on the Lord Jesus Christ, and make
not provision for the flesh, to fulfil the lusts thereof.**

Romans 13:14

This may look as though it's an unusual text for teaching on extraordinary things; but there's a phrase here that I want you to catch, because I hope it will arrest your thinking as it did mine. Notice the phrase, **make not provision for the flesh.**

Notice who's making provision for the flesh here. You and I. And Paul is admonishing us to stop that. If we make provision for the flesh, then we're going to end up in sin. We're going to end up fulfilling our lusts. We're going to end up assisting Satan in creating opportunities for us to compromise.

The Amplified Bible says it this way: **But clothe yourself with the Lord Jesus Christ, the Messiah, and make no provision for [indulging] the flesh.** Then it tells us how we stop making provision to fulfill the flesh: **Put a stop to thinking about the evil cravings of your physical nature—to [gratify its] desires (lusts).** Again, notice the phrase, **put a stop to thinking about...evil cravings.**

To me, this means that making provision for the flesh has everything to do with the way I think. It means that my thoughts have everything to do with making provision for sin.

Advanced Preparation

Before we go on, I want to define the word *provision* as it is used in this verse. It means "forethought,"[1] "preparation,"[2] or "a measure taken in advance."[3] The word *forethought* is defined as "advanced deliberation or consideration."[4]

Now, for the lack of a better illustration, let me use this one: If you were to fantasize about an illicit sexual affair to the point that it was consuming your thoughts, then eventually you're going to make provision for fulfilling that fantasy. I've known people who have done that.

I knew a man who, as far as I knew, was truly sold out to God and loved the Word of Faith.

But after a while, I began to notice a change in him. I noticed that he wasn't listening to Christian teaching tapes or Christian music anymore. He even started dressing differently. He tried to look younger and more "worldly."

I'm talking about a man my age, a man in his early fifties. So apparently he was making provision for something.

Now, I didn't know at the time that he'd already been planning to divorce his wife, but I knew something was wrong. After all, when a man who has been very conservative all of his life suddenly starts wearing loud-colored clothes, getting a dark tan, wearing a gold chain around his neck and trying to look "cool," you can tell he's making provision for a change in lifestyle. And Satan was setting him up. In fact, the man was assisting Satan in setting himself up. Why? He's making provision. Well, it was no surprise when we discovered that he had gone back into the world and wanted no part of a Christian lifestyle.

Provision for Both Negative and Positive

Now, if you can make provision for something negative in your life, would it be unreasonable for me to say that you can also make provision for something positive? For example, when a man and his wife discover that she has conceived and is with child, what is the next thing they do? Of course, they start making provision for that child. They begin talking about turning the extra bedroom into a nursery. They shop for a baby crib and baby clothes. The husband goes out and buys a set of boxing gloves because he wants his kid to be the next heavyweight champion of the world—even if the baby is a girl.

So in Romans 13:14, Paul is telling us that you can cause negative things as well as positive things to happen in your life as a result of your making provision for them. And the primary way that you make provision for them is by allowing your thought life to be consumed by whatever it is that you hope will happen. The principle Paul is expressing is this: Your life tends to go in the direction of your most dominant thoughts. Whatever you think about the most, that's the direction your life will go.

The Reasons Why

So our thoughts can dictate our outcome. And here's what the Spirit of God said to me when I was asking Him why I was not experiencing as many extraordinary things as I had during the first part of that year: He said, *It's because you're not as consumed with it as you were. You don't think as much about it as you did then. You're not talking about it like you did then. In fact, you're not even preaching about it anymore. You haven't preached a sermon in several meetings about the extraordinary.*

And then He told me why I had stopped preaching about the extraordinary. He said, *You thought you needed new material for television.* I thought I had to come up with a new sermon in order to keep my audience watching my program. I should have known better.

One time, somebody asked Rev. Kenneth Hagin, Sr., "Are you going to preach Mark 11:23-24 every service? Don't you know anything else?"

Brother Hagin said, "When you get this, we'll move on to something new."

I should have remembered this and just kept on preaching, teaching, declaring and expecting the extraordinary. God always confirms His word with signs following. Mark 16:20 declares, **And they went forth and preached every where, the Lord working with them, and confirming the word with signs following.**

Listen Like You've Never Heard It Before

Years ago, the Lord told me to go back and listen to the seven messages that I first heard Brother Copeland preach back in 1969. We didn't have cassettes then; they were reel-to-reel tapes. In fact, I still have them, and I still have the old reel-to-reel tape player that someone gave me so I could listen to those messages back then.

I set the player up on my desk in my study, and I listened to the very first message that I had ever heard Kenneth Copeland preach, a message entitled "The Word of Faith." The Lord had said to me, *I want you to listen to this message like you've never heard it before. Just shut your mind down for a moment and act as though this is the first time you've ever heard this. Here's why—I want it to do on the inside of you the very same thing it did the first time you ever heard it.*

So, I sat there listening to that reel-to-reel tape like I'd never heard it before. I thought I'd heard everything on those tapes at least one hundred times. But here I was listening to them again years later, and I heard Brother Copeland say some things that I had not heard him say before. I got just as excited as I did the first time I heard him preach.

Right in the middle of my excitement the telephone rang, and it was Brother Copeland. He said, "What are you doing?"

I said, "I'm listening to you preach."

He said, "What am I preaching?"

I said, "I'm listening to the very first sermon that I ever heard you preach back in 1969, and I'm telling you, this message is so anointed and so powerful that it's doing to me right now what it did to me back then."

He said, "Well, when you finish it, get that tape over here. I need to hear it myself."

The Bible says that faith comes by *hearing*. (Rom. 10:17.) It doesn't say faith comes by *having heard*. You need to hear it more than once. Don't ever think that once is enough.

"Again I Say..."

Who said we have to come up with something new all the time? Haven't you noticed how many times Jesus said, "And *again* I say unto you..."? I asked Him one time, "Why did You have the same story written in Matthew, Mark, Luke and John?"

He said, *Because I knew you wouldn't get it in one.* Don't laugh. Some of you still haven't got it.

"Again I say unto you...." That makes me wonder how many times He had already said it.

Now, if you look at the people that He was talking to—His disciples—then no wonder He had to say it again. Have you ever read John 14 through 17? You will find that Jesus is giving His disciples a wonderful discourse on His relationship with the Father. He says things like, "I and My Father are one." "If you've seen Me, you've seen the Father." He said, "The Father within Me—He doeth the works."

He spent several chapters talking about his relationship with the Father. And when he got through, Philip said, "Show us the Father."

Do you know what Jesus said? "Philip, how long am I going to have to be with you?"

Don't laugh, because some of Philip's descendants are probably reading this book.

So when I asked the Lord why I was not receiving as many extraordinary things as I had, He said to me: *Son, when you stopped talking about it, when you stopped thinking about it and when you stopped preaching about it, you also stopped making provision for it.*

Well, I immediately began correcting this situation. I became consumed with it once again and expected it to happen, and I was not disappointed. I want extraordinary things happening in my life every day, and I want them happening to you as well.

Miracles Are Coming Your Way

As I have previously stated, if we want extraordinary, rare and uncommon events to happen to us, then we have to make provision for them. We can't just sit passively by and wait for God to do it for us.

Brother Oral Roberts says that miracles are coming your way every day. However, there are a lot of people who do not enjoy miracles every day. It seems that miracles pass most people by. Is it because God's a respecter of persons? No, it's not. Or could it be because they haven't made provision for them? Why is it that some people seem to be more blessed than others? Could it be that some people make provision for them more so than others? Since God is no respecter of persons, it isn't His fault if some people receive miracles and others don't. In other words, the responsibility is ours.

Talk About It

When God speaks a *rhema* word, or a living, spoken word, into your spirit, He expects you to make that word the most dominant thought in your thinking. He expects you to get up thinking about it. He expects you to spend the day thinking about it. He expects you to go to bed thinking about it.

What you think about is what you're going to talk about. Consequently, if God is going to expect you to think about it when you get up, think about it during the day and think about it when you go to bed, then He's also going to expect you to talk about it.

This principle is clearly stated in the Bible:

> **Now these are the commandments, the statutes, and the judgments, which the Lord your God commanded to teach you, that ye might do them in the land whither ye go to possess it: and these words, which I command thee this day, shall be in thine heart: and thou shalt teach them diligently unto thy children, and shalt talk of them when thou sittest in thine house, and when**

**thou walkest by the way, and when thou liest
down, and when thou risest up.**

Deuteronomy 6:1,6,7

Notice he said, "The words that I give you, I want you
to talk about them when you sit down; I want you to talk
about them when you get up; I want you to teach them
to your children. I want you to talk about them wherever
you go." Now what happens when you are constantly
talking about something? You become consumed with it.
What happens when you are consumed with it? It has an
effect on your attitude. You will begin to expect those
things to come to pass in your life.

If you get up every morning thinking, *This is the day
that God is going to do extraordinary things in my life.
This is the day that God will meet my needs in uncommon
and unusual ways,* then there is no way that you can be
depressed. What happens to your expectancy? It's high!
What are you doing? You're making provision. I like to say
it this way: You've given God something to work with.
God wants to bless you, but you have to give Him something to work with.

What Do You Have?

Do you remember the widow in 2 Kings who came to the prophet Elisha seeking a solution to her problem of great debt? Let's look at that story again because it is such a wonderful example of making provision for the extraordinary by giving God something to work with.

> Now there cried a certain woman of the wives of the sons of the prophets unto Elisha, saying, Thy servant my husband is dead; and thou knowest that thy servant did fear the Lord: and the creditor is come to take unto him my two sons to be bondmen.
>
> And Elisha said unto her, What shall I do for thee? tell me, what hast thou in the house? And she said, Thine handmaid hath not any thing in the house, save a pot of oil.
>
> Then he said, Go, borrow thee vessels abroad of all thy neighbours, even empty vessels; borrow not a few. And when thou art come in, thou shalt shut the door upon thee and upon thy sons, and shalt pour out into all those vessels, and thou shalt set aside that which is full.

So she went from him, and shut the door upon her and upon her sons, who brought the vessels to her; and she poured out.

And it came to pass, when the vessels were full, that she said unto her son, Bring me yet a vessel. And he said unto her, There is not a vessel more. And the oil stayed.

Then she came and told the man of God. And he said, Go, sell the oil, and pay thy debt, and live thou and thy children of the rest.

2 Kings 4:1-7

Once again, God needed something to work with before He could do the miraculous in her life. Notice that the prophet said, "What do you have?"

It's like when God asked Moses at the Red Sea, *What do you have?*

Moses said, "A stick."

God said, in effect, *I can work with that. Stretch it out over the water.* (Exo. 14:16.)

Like Moses, you have something. Let God have it. God just needs something to work with.

This widow didn't think she had anything. All she had was a little pot of oil. Well, look what God did when she took what she had—even though in her mind it looked as though she didn't have anything. In the mind of God it was something to work with. He multiplied the oil and met her need.

The Prophet's Chamber

In that same chapter is another story of a woman who made provision for the extraordinary by giving God something to work with.

And it fell on a day, that Elisha passed to Shunem, where was a great woman; and she constrained him to eat bread. And so it was, that as oft as he passed by, he turned in thither to eat bread.

And she said unto her husband, Behold now, I perceive that this is an holy man of God, which passeth by us continually. Let us make a little chamber, I pray thee, on the wall; and let us set for him there a bed, and a table, and a stool, and

a candlestick: and it shall be, when he cometh to
us, that he shall turn in thither.

2 Kings 4:8-10

Now, what did this woman do? She made provision. She perceived that this was a holy man of God. She perceived that this was a man who was a representative of the Most High God, and everywhere this man went, extraordinary events followed him. So she said, "Let's make provision for the extraordinary. Let's build a prophet's chamber. Let's build a little room here so every time this man passes by, he'll be able to come and stay in this room. We'll put a bed, a table, a chair and a candle in there, and every time he passes by, he can rest here." What was she doing? She was making provision for the extraordinary.

Did you notice what happened when she made provision for something extraordinary?

And it fell on a day, that he came thither, and
he turned into the chamber, and lay there. And
he said to Gehazi his servant, Call this
Shunammite. And when he had called her, she
stood before him. And he said unto him, Say now
unto her, Behold, thou hast been careful for us
with all this care; what is to be done for thee?

wouldest thou be spoken for to the king, or to the captain of the host? And she answered, I dwell among mine own people.

And he said, What then is to be done for her? And Gehazi answered, Verily she hath no child, and her husband is old.

2 Kings 4:11-14

The prophet of God asks, "What would you like? Is there anything we can do for you?"

Now he is God's representative. She had made provision for the man of God. He wants to do something for her in return. So his servant answered that the one thing the woman needed was a child.

And he said, Call her. And when he had called her, she stood in the door. And he said, About this season, according to the time of life, thou shalt embrace a son.

And she said, Nay, my Lord, thou man of God, do not lie unto thine handmaid.

And the woman conceived, and bare a son at that season that Elisha had said unto her, according to the time of life.

2 Kings 4:15-17

Do you think this would have happened to her had she not built that chamber in her house? The Bible says Elisha walked by there continually. In other words, if she hadn't made provision, the extraordinary would have passed her by.

Don't Let It Pass You By

If she had not given God something to work with, the extraordinary would have passed her by just as it did to the Pharisees and the doctors of the law who came to hear Jesus preach in Luke 5. The Bible says, **The power of the Lord was present to heal them** (Luke 5:17), but not one of them was healed. Miracles were coming their way, and not one of them received one. Why? *They didn't make provision for it.* These religious leaders were not there to receive; they were there to criticize. They were there trying to trap Jesus. They didn't make provision for the supernatural, and it passed them by.

However, there was a person who did get healed that day. He was an outsider brought in by some of his friends. They were so determined to receive the extraordinary that they tore the roof off the house where Jesus was and lowered this sick man down right in front of Him. When Jesus saw their faith, the man was healed. (Luke 5:17-26.)

Why? Because they had made provision for the extraordinary. By their faith and by their actions, they had given Jesus something to work with. And that's exactly what you must do to make provision for the extraordinary in your life: By your faith and by your actions, you must give God something to work with! When you do, you won't be disappointed.

Chapter 8

Conclusion: There's No Way To Stop It

L et me conclude this book by telling you about an experience that I had. This story illustrates how faith with corresponding actions can bring an extraordinary, rare and uncommon blessing into your life.

Years ago, when I left Brother Copeland's organization to launch out into my ministry, I drove a 1973 Ford station wagon from one end of this nation to the other in order to preach in the various cities where I had been invited.

One day, the Spirit of God spoke to me and said, *I want you to start believing for an airplane for your ministry.*

Well, that sounded to me like the most foolish thing I'd ever heard in my life. What in the world did I need an airplane for? I had plenty of meetings, but it wasn't like there was a great demand for an airplane. Besides that, I didn't even know how to fly an airplane. I would have looked foolish driving down the highway at 55 miles an hour in an airplane!

But God said, *No, you don't need it now, but there will come a time when you'll not be able to fulfill what I've called you to do without one. Don't wait until the demand is there—do it now while there's no pressure; start believing for it now.*

He added, *And I don't want you borrowing any money for it. I don't want you having any debt on it.*

Well, I said okay, even though at the time I didn't see how this could ever happen. My wife and I, our two daughters and my two staff members all joined together and believed God to provide our ministry with an airplane.

Acting Like It

Well, as I said, I didn't need one right then. But you know, it seemed that after we prayed, the demand on my ministry increased, and I couldn't get everywhere that I was asked to preach by driving. One day the Spirit of God said, *Do you really believe that you received that airplane when you prayed,* according to Mark 11:24?

I said, "I do. I believe I received it when I prayed."

He asked, *Then why aren't you acting like it?*

"Lord, how does one act like he has an airplane? What could I possibly do to act like I have an airplane?"

Didn't I say faith without works is dead? Didn't I say faith without corresponding actions is void of power?

I said, "Yes, but how do you act like you have an airplane?"

Well, how would it affect your schedule if you had an airplane right now?

"Well, I could go to more of the places where I've been invited to preach" I said.

He said, *I thought you said that you believed you received?*

"I do."

Then why aren't you accepting more of these invitations?

"I can't get there driving."

He said, *I thought you said that you believed you received?*

"I do."

Then why aren't you acting like it?

Finally, I asked, "What do You want me to do?"

He said, *Why don't you set up your schedule as if you have an airplane?*

So I said, "Okay."

Doing My Part

Well, in my office at that time was a man who handled all of my invitations and set up all of my meetings.

I said to him, "I want you to accept every invitation that has come into this office. I want you to book me up so tight that there is absolutely no way that I can get there in an automobile."

Now, he drove the van that we carried the tapes and the sound system in, and he said, "Well, how am I going to get there?"

I said, "Well, you'll just have to make all the meetings that you can since you won't be able to drive to every one."

He said, "Oh, okay."

So he started calling all these people who had invited me to come. Once the dates were set, he gave me a copy of the itinerary. I was in New York one night, Los Angeles the next and Miami after that. There was no way I could get to all these places in a Ford station wagon.

I thought, *All right, I've done my part. Where's the airplane?*

No airplane. No money for an airplane. Nothing. I mean, there was not a sign of an airplane.

I said, "God, You told me to do this. Where's the airplane?"

He said, *You just keep your word and make all these meetings.*

I said, "Well, how am I going to get there?"

He said, *By airplane.*

I said, "Well, where is it?"

He said, *Don't you believe that you received it when you prayed? Why aren't you thanking Me for it?*

He said, *If you wait until you see it before you begin thanking Me for it, then that's not faith. Start thanking Me now—I'm working behind the scenes.*

The Next Step: A Hangar

So now the only thing that I could do was to fly on the commercial airlines. However, sometimes there were no commercial airlines going to some of the places where I was preaching. Therefore, I had to fly to the city as close to the place as I could, rent a car and then drive the rest of the way. And I was doing this day in and day out.

Now, you would have thought that with all these corresponding actions that an airplane would have manifested within the next week. But it didn't!

I did this month after month after month. Then God had the audacity to ask me again, *Do you really believe that you received that airplane?*

I said, "Yes."

He said, *Then, why aren't you acting like it?*

I said, "God, what else could I possibly do to act like I have an airplane?"

Where do you plan to keep it? You don't park an airplane in your backyard, son, He said.

"Well, you keep them at an airport?"

Where? He said.

"In a hangar."

Have you got a hangar? He said.

"No, you can't have a hangar until you get an airplane."

Then you don't really believe you have received it, He said.

"God, I believe I received it."

Then why aren't you making provision for it? Go to the airport and rent a hangar, He said.

So I went to the airport in Fort Worth to see about renting a hangar for the airplane that I believed I had received. I'd never talked to anybody about a hangar before. I didn't know what I was doing. So, I walked into the office and said, "I'd like to talk to someone about renting a hangar."

They took me to another office, and this man started asking me questions. After writing down my name, he asked, "And what kind of airplane do you have?"

I said, "A good one. You know, with wings and engines and propellers and radios and—it's a good one."

"Well, what kind is it?"

"Well, I don't really know."

"Oh, you're not the pilot?"

"Oh, no, I'm not the pilot. I'm just the owner."

"But you don't know what kind of airplane you have?"

I said, "Well, I haven't seen it yet."

"Well," he said, "we can't rent you a hangar if you don't already have an airplane. We've got people on a waiting list who already have airplanes."

I said, "Sir, you don't understand. I won't get an airplane until I have a hangar."

He said, "I've never heard anything like that."

I said, "Well, you don't know my Boss. He works a little differently than most people. He said that I won't get an airplane until I have a hangar. You've got to rent a hangar to me, or I won't get an airplane."

He said, "Well, that's not the way we normally do things. This is uncommon."

I said, "Well, I understand that, but you've got to let me have a hangar, because I've got to have a place to put it before I can have it."

He said, "Well, when do you expect it?"

I said, "I'm expecting it any day."

He said, "What's the holdup?"

I said, "A hangar."

He didn't want to give me a hangar. But I finally convinced him to let me have one. So he assigned me a hangar and then asked me to give him a total of $160 to cover two months' rent. So, then I had a hangar with nothing in it!

A Good One!

I was doing what God told me to do. I was making provision. I bought a lock, and then I went to see my hangar.

As I was looking at it, the man with the hangar next door came over and introduced himself.

He said, "Welcome to Meacham Field. What kind of airplane are you flying?"

I said, "A good one!"

"A good one? Yeah, what is it?"

"I don't know, but it's a good one. Praise God."

Well, he didn't talk to me very long. He evidently thought I was some kind of nut, but all I was doing is what God told me to do.

God's Working Behind the Scenes

Now, you would have thought that the airplane would have showed up before dark. But it didn't.

I drove out to my hangar every day when I was in town. I even put some things in it. I put in polishing cloths, wax and a water hose so I could wash my airplane. I put my tool chest in there. I was ready. All I needed was an airplane.

Conclusion: There's No Way To Stop It

What was I doing? Making provision. You see, just like the Shunammite woman, I built a chamber. And do you know what happened? God came through before I had to pay another month's rent on that hangar.

Carolyn and I were in a meeting in Omaha, Nebraska, with Fred and Betty Price, and as soon as that meeting was over, we all went to the airport to catch commercial flights back to our homes. Carolyn and I were on a flight to Dallas, and Fred and Betty were taking a flight back to California. We told them goodbye, and they started walking toward their gate and we started walking toward ours. Then it hit me. I don't know how to describe it, but it just hit me that somehow, someway, my airplane was on its way.

I turned around and shouted at Brother Fred, "Fred! Hey, Fred!"

He was walking down the corridor, but when he heard me, he turned around and yelled, "Yeah, what is it?"

I shouted, "I just wanted you to hear me say it—I've got my own airplane in the name of Jesus!"

He shouted back, "I believe it, brother!"

When Carolyn and I arrived in Dallas, my General Manager met us at the airport and handed me a note from some people we knew. It said, "Please call us when you get home; we want you to have dinner with us tonight in Dallas."

So, we met them that evening at a restaurant in Dallas. I hadn't even taken the first bite of my food yet, when they said, "We invited you to dinner tonight because God has been dealing with us about giving you our airplane. We couldn't do it before now because we owed money on it, and we were believing God to pay it off before we gave it to you. But tonight we want to tell you that God has given us the money to pay off the debt, and here are the keys and the title to your airplane."

It was then that I understood what God meant when He said, *I'm working behind the scenes.* You see, all that time that I was making provision, even though it looked as if nothing was happening, God was working behind the scenes. However, I had to cooperate with Him by taking uncommon and unusual measures in order to make provision for the extraordinary.

A Warning

As I've said all along, my purpose in this book is to show you how you can bring the extraordinary into your life. I've told you about some of my own experiences so you could see the faithfulness of God. However, let me warn you: don't do something that I did just because I did it. Don't do something Brother Copeland or Brother Hagin or Brother Roberts did just because they did it.

For instance, don't you go out and rent a hangar because you're believing for an airplane *unless God told you to do it*. You do what *God* tells you to do, not what He told *someone else* to do.

The Bible says there were seven men who decided that they could do what Paul did. They wanted to cast out devils, so they found a demon-possessed man and said, "In the name of Jesus Christ of Nazareth whom Paul preaches, come out of him."

The demons spoke up and said, "Jesus we know, and Paul we know; but who are you?" And then they beat those boys up and tore their clothes off of them. (Acts 19:13-16.)

I always like to say that the moral to that story is this: You can lose your clothes trying to live on somebody else's revelation.

So, when I say "make provision for the extraordinary," you're going to have to listen to God to find out what He wants you to do specifically. God told me what I needed to do to make provision for an airplane. I didn't do it because somebody else did it.

Your corresponding actions have to be inspired by the Holy Ghost. If you don't get this important revelation, you'll probably get into trouble.

The extraordinary belongs to you! God wants to do unusual things in your life every day. I trust that the lessons which I've shared in this book will put you in position to experience them as never before.

ENDNOTES

Introduction

[1] Vine, s.v. "prophecy," p. 492.

[2] Ibid.

Chapter 1

[1] *Websters New Twentieth Century Dictionary*, p. 651.

[2] Ibid.

Chapter 3

[1] Funk and Wagnalls, s.v. "extraordinary."

[2] Ibid.

[3] Ibid.

[4] Ibid.

[5] Ibid.

[6] Ibid.

Chapter 4

[1] Vine, s.v. "elect," p. 196.

[2] Vine, s.v. "peculiar," p. 477.

Chapter 6

[1] *Websters New Twentieth Century Dictionary*, p. 1538.

Chapter 7

[1] Vine, s.v. "provision," pp. 495, 496.

[2] Ibid.

[3] *Websters New Twentieth Century Dictionary*, p. 1440.

[4] *American Dictionary of the English Language*, s.v. "forethought."

REFERENCES

Funk and Wagnalls. *New Comprehensive International Dictionary.*

Vine, W.E. *Expository Dictionary of Biblical Words.* Nashville: Thomas Nelson, Inc., 1985.

Webster, Noah. *American Dictionary of the English Language.* New York: S. Converse, 1828..

Webster's New Twentieth Century Dictionary, 2nd ed. New York: Simon & Schuster, Inc., 1979.

ABOUT THE AUTHOR

Jerry Savelle is a noted author, evangelist and teacher, who travels extensively throughout the United Sates, Canada and around the globe. He is president of Jerry Savelle Ministries International, a ministry of many outreaches devoted to meeting the needs of believers all over the world.

Well known for his balanced biblical teaching, Dr. Savelle has conducted seminars, crusades and conventions for over twenty-five years, as well as ministered in thousands of churches and fellowships. He is in great demand today because of his inspiring message of victory and faith and his vivid, often humorous, illustrations from the Bible. He teaches the uncompromising Word of God with a power and an authority that is exciting but with a love that delivers the message directly to the spirit man.

In addition to his international headquarters in Crowley, Texas, Dr. Savelle is also founder of JSMI-Kenya; JSMI-United Kingdom; JSMI-South Africa; JSMI-Australia; and JSMI-Tanzania. In 1994, he established the JSMI Bible Institute and School of World Evangelism. It is a two-year school for the preparation of ministers to take the Gospel of Jesus Christ to the nations of the world.

The missions outreach of his ministry extends to over fifty countries around the world. JSMI further ministers the Word of God through its prison ministry outreach.

Dr. Savelle has authored many books and has an extensive video and cassette teaching-tape ministry and a worldwide television broadcast. Thousands of books, tapes and videos are distributed around the world each year through Jerry Savelle Ministries International.

To contact Jerry Savelle,

write:

Jerry Savelle

P.O. Box 748

Crowley, Texas 76036

Please include your prayer requests

and comments when you write.

OTHER BOOKS BY JERRY SAVELLE

Seizing God-Given Opportunities

Are You Tired of Sowing Much?

Force of Joy

Honoring Your Heritage of Faith

If Satan Can't Steal Your Joy

Right Mental Attitude

Sharing Jesus Effectively

The Established Heart

Turning Your Adversity Into Victory

You Can Have Abundant Life

Available from your local bookstore.

HARRISON HOUSE
Tulsa, Oklahoma 74153

PRAYER OF SALVATION

A born-again, committed relationship with God is the key to the victorious life. Jesus, the Son of God, laid down His life and rose again so that we could spend eternity with Him in heaven and experience His absolute best on earth. The Bible says, **For God so loved the world, that he gave his only begotten Son, that whosoever believeth in him should not perish, but have everlasting life** (John 3:16).

It is the will of God that everyone receive eternal salvation. The way to receive this salvation is to call upon the name of Jesus and confess Him as your Lord. The Bible says, **That if thou shalt confess with thy mouth the Lord Jesus, and shalt believe in thine heart that God hath raised him from the dead, thou shalt be saved. For whosoever shall call upon the name of the Lord shall be saved** (Romans 10:9-10,13).

Jesus has given salvation, healing and countless benefits to all who call upon His name. These benefits can be yours if you receive Him into your heart by praying this prayer.

Father,

I come to you right now as a sinner. Right now, I choose to turn away from sin, and I ask you to cleanse me of all unrighteousness. I believe that your Son, Jesus, died on the cross to take away my sins. I also believe that He rose again from the dead so that I might be justified and made righteous through faith in Him. I call upon the name of Jesus Christ for salvation. I want Him to be the Savior and Lord of my life. Jesus, I choose to follow You, and ask that You fill me with the power of the Holy Spirit. I declare that right now, I am a born-again child of God. I am free from sin, and full of the righteousness of God. I am saved in Jesus' name, Amen.

If you have prayed this prayer to receive Jesus Christ into your life, we would like to hear from you. Please write us at:

Harrison House

P.O. Box 35035

Tulsa, Oklahoma 74153

THE HARRISON HOUSE VISION

Proclaiming the truth and the power

Of the Gospel of Jesus Christ

With excellence;

Challenging Christians to

Live victoriously,

Grow spiritually,

Know God intimately.